Colleen Thankyou for
your support!

The best is yet to come.

Wilson

FUN IS MY FAVOURITE
F-WORD
A COMEDIC PERSONAL DEVELOPMENT BOOK ABOUT HOW TO HAVE FUN AND MAKE MONEY
WILSON WONG

Fun is my Favourite F-Word

"This is a comedic personal development book about how to have fun and make money based on events that happened in my life."

Wilson Wong

ISBN: 978-1-9992291-0-8

Louis Hebert - Art & Cover

Scott Ironmonger - Editing & Format

This book is dedicated to all the people out there willing to sacrifice and overcome life's challenges to live their dreams.

I thought it would be fun to write a book.
Here it is. Enjoy responsibly.

Table of Contents:

Preface

Wow, thanks for picking up my book. I really appreciate the love and support. Honestly, I had no expectations when I was writing this book. I'm a simple man. I wrote this book because I thought it would be funny. Let me elaborate.

"How funny would it be if I wrote a book and became an author?"

Yup, that was my thought process.

My friends know me as silly, high energy, and unpredictable, but good unpredictable, not the "SURPRISE! I got chu pregnant" kind.

The fact that me, Wilson Wong (it's the preface, I'm allowed to talk in the third person about myself, and it's my book), wrote a book would be the biggest surprise to my friends and family because they have no idea what I'm doing.

I am not an academic, I was actually a subpar student. At best I was B-minus, like my blood type. I did go to university and graduate with a $30,000 piece of paper saying, "Good job, you're competent enough-ish." What was my degree in? It was a Bachelor of Arts with a Major in Psychology and a Minor in Business. What's my occupation? I'm in sales.

I didn't graduate university in the standard four years. I did it in five because the government didn't want to lend me any more money. I think this book is hilarious because when I was in university I sucked at writing to the point that I needed my girlfriend (at the time) to literally write my papers for me.

The way I talk is also the way I write. From here on out, you'll probably get a chance to feel me out, get to know who I am and if I ever get a chance to meet you, you'll be like, "Oh, he really does talk like he writes." In this case I'm talking to you through many pieces of paper.

So…….

Here is the TL;DR (Too Long; Didn't Read) version: if you make a lot of money but you're not having a lot of fun, or you're having TOO much fun but you're just scraping by, then this book is for you. But if you're making a ton of money AND you're having fun then you don't need to read this book. You're living it. Congratulations.

What did I write about? This is a personal development book on how to have fun and make money. How to literally monetize fun. Each chapter has a lesson and it's based on real events that happened in my life.

Why did I write this book? I just wanted to show people what fun can be like. My definition of fun changes from activity to activity, mood to mood. If you're like some of my friends, you might be a little stuck, unsure of how to get the most out of your day. Even if you are having fun, you may wonder, "How much more fun could I have?"

Maybe you have a great job and you're good at it but you're not really having any fun. Sure, you might have the big expensive toys, that sexy luxury car and even that perfect white picket fence kind of home. Yet, you come back to your expensive car and big ass house and you loathe the next day. Why? Doesn't money buy happiness?

There's this idea that when you make a lot of money, you're not allowed to have fun or be spontaneous. Sure, a weekend or two out might be fun, but if you're honest with yourself, isn't that just temporary escapism? If you literally live for Friday and Saturday and need Sunday to "recharge" for the dreaded Monday, I think you're just covering up the real issue. The fact that you are having fun two out of seven days a week is haunting.

Let's do some napkin math. There are 365 days in a year and you live for the weekends (two days). That literally means you're having fun 28% of the time for the rest of your life. It also means you hate (insert any synonym) your life 72% of the time. You dread it. Are you telling me you want to live this way for the next 65+ years of your life? That's fucked up.

Here's the thing.....

You spent all your time in school trying to get a perfect grade. Yet, you are failing REAL LIFE. You have a D-minus.

This is scary to me. Personally, I don't think "failing" at life is fun at all. But the only way to stop failing is by recognizing that you are failing. Then the only way is up, right? And I hope by reading my book you'll learn to look at your failures more creatively. Because the more creative you get, the more fun you can recognize in every situation, even if it sucks. It might be a struggle to start with, but at least you'll know where you're at and where you can go.

On the flip side, there's also an issue if you are having too much fun. Sure, you're popular, you're the life of the party, and when you walk into a room people know the night just got better because you're there. However, you literally slave away paycheque to paycheque because you don't want to get "tied down" to a schedule. You make barely any money. The drugs, alcohol, and experiences are incredible in the moment, but there is no purpose to your life.

Even if you have a significant other, how sustainable is that? At the end of the day, after all the fun is had, you're still by yourself. You see your friends move forward, "grow up", move out of their parents' basement, buy their first home, get engaged and, in some, cases raise a family. But here you are partying and "having fun." You can deflect the real issue here. You're scared that if you got a "real" job, all the fun you're having would be gone. You would have to conform, be a real adult in the "real" world. So, you suppress that feeling.

What now?

There is this problem that if we make money, we aren't having fun. But if we have too much fun, we don't make enough to keep it sustainable and practical.

This book merges money and fun together. The more you enjoy yourself at whatever you do, the more able you will be to monetize it later on.

Please note, if you decide on the money route, the fun will be delayed; if you decide on fun first, the money will come later.

This book will share how I achieved both at "speed."

Again, I just want to thank all of you for supporting me. This book was really fun to write. There were long days and late nights writing. For me, this is just a really expensive journal and a glorified diary. Enjoy my stories, but take them with a grain of salt. Or, if you're really hungry, treat it like a buffet: take what you want and leave what you don't want.

This is a story about my upbringing and how my environment and circumstances shaped who I am today.

Chapter One:

Survival of the Kindest

Like most of you, probably, my story begins with my parents. They came to Canada from Vietnam but are actually Chinese because my grandparents moved to Vietnam. When the Vietnam War broke out my mom and dad had to escape from the country. After that they travelled over much of Asia as displaced people. Then, at some point in the 70's, they came to Canada.

Here's the kicker: my parents didn't know each other when they landed. Both were in their late teens when they met in Canada. My dad was working as a waiter at a Chinese restaurant and my mom was working there as a waitress. It was inevitable their paths would cross. They hooked up, got married, and a few years later my brother was born. Six years after that, I popped out.

I was born at Edmonton's Royal Alexandra Hospital in 1989. Back then, the city had a population of less than a million people (that's roughly a quarter of the population of Los Angeles, or the number of residents in the average one-bedroom apartment in Beijing). Many of those people were Asian immigrants too. Chinese, Vietnamese, Laos, Filipinos; you name 'em, we got 'em.

There were two elementary schools near my home, J.A. Fife and Kildare. Kildare would have been a 30-minute walk away, but J.A. Fife was just across the street and one alley away from our home. To me there was a massive difference between them though: Kildare had a Chinese Immersion program, J.A. Fife didn't. Naturally, I ended up going to J.A. Fife.

At J.A. Fife I was one of just a handful of Asian students going to a predominantly white school. That meant the friends I made were all white. As a result, I learned a lot about white culture, mannerisms, and even food. It wasn't rice and veggies; it was meat and potatoes or pasta. The way kids were disciplined was different too. In Chinese culture you would never talk back. Being hit as a kid was normal, whereas it is frowned upon in Western culture.

My parents never had time to absorb Western culture, or pop culture, so growing up with them meant I was immersed in Eastern values at home and surrounded by Western values elsewhere. I didn't know what sports Canada played. What even were "sports?" I had no idea what hockey, soccer, baseball, or football were.

I was born into a typical poor immigrant family. My mom cleaned tables and toilets, my dad waited tables. There was not much glamour there. I went to an elementary school every day where I stood out like a sore thumb. Then, every Saturday, I went to Chinese school at 8:00 am, and every Sunday we'd go to Chinese Temple because there was food served after prayer.

The temple also acted as a daycare and babysitting service. And if we couldn't be at the school or temple, my dad would take us to the restaurant where he worked and our nice "aunties" and "uncles" would look after us. Before my brother and I could play in the restaurant, my dad would have us set tables, dry chopsticks, and keep things neat and tidy. We were the best type of child labour: free.

When it comes to Chinese food, here is my best biased advice. The best Chinese food comes from these three trade secrets. Once you've recognised and tried it, you'll never look back.

Number One: The restaurant has been shut down by the health inspector at least twice in a year. The dirtier the Chinese restaurant the more authentic it is. That's facts.

Number Two: When you walk in you need to see children playing at one corner table that customers have never used. Also you need to look out for their babysitter who is "the grandma." The kids will be watched by the oldest-looking human being in the world. She's so old that she takes her time to breath. (Bonus tip: the older the grandma looks, the deeper the roots that restaurant has.)

Last but not least, Number Three: The parking lot lines are just there for show. Whenever you try to park in front of a Chinese restaurant, you usually can't because the patrons need maximum space for exiting their vehicle. You will usually have to park across the street and then walk to the restaurant.

When you see these three things at a Chinese restaurant you will know that it's the best in the city.

When we weren't free labour at the restaurant or getting free daycare at the temple, my brother and I mainly grew up at our aunt's house. So, you see, we barely even lived at home. All my parents did was work, work, work. My mom would drop us off at our aunt's when she had to go to school or do a night shift. Nothing out of the ordinary there for a surviving immigrant family. But we still found ways to have fun.

My favourite "sport" in elementary school was soccer-baseball, a kind of dumbed-down version of baseball for uncoordinated kids. Instead of using a bat to hit a small hard white ball, you kick a large red rubber ball. The "pitcher" rolls the ball towards you and your job is to not Charlie Brown it and fall on your ass.

Another sport I learned in elementary school was Red Ass. All you need for this game is a ball and a wall. The rules of Red Ass are simple: you throw a tennis ball against a wall and another kid has to catch it after it bounces. Then they throw it back at the wall. You alternate catching and throwing until someone messes up. If you attempt to catch the ball and you fumble it or it touches you, your ass is literally on the line. You immediately have to run and touch the wall to be "safe" while behind you the other players run towards the ball, grab it, and attempt to hit the wall before you touch it. If the ball gets to the wall before you do, you're the Red Ass. Then you have to face the wall, bend over, and present your ass while the other kids throw the ball at it from a distance. If they hit it, you're out.

If you grew up in a North American household, maybe you dreamed of playing in the NHL or the NFL. The best I could hope for as an ignorant Chinese kid was to be a professional Red Ass player. That wouldn't hold up though, because first, my parents would have zero clue what that means, and second, there's no such thing as a professional league for Red Ass. If you googled "Professional Red Ass" you'd probably get some sort of spanking-type porn site, but I wouldn't know.

I never made it in pro Red Ass, but I've got no regrets.

The biggest challenge for my parents was the family finances. It was extremely difficult to send my brother and I into organized sports. Hockey, soccer, and other clubs were expensive because of memberships, uniforms, and equipment costs.

This one time my mom got me a pair of ice skates and took me to a local outdoor ice rink. We thought that since it was outside it would be free and you could just show up and start skating. My mom dropped me off and I strapped on my skates and went onto the ice. As I was skating around an old guy came up and started yelling at me to get off because I didn't have a special skate tag that meant I could use the rink. Yes, I got kicked off an ice rink at six years old. To this day I still don't know how to ice skate. That old man ended my skating career. What a dick.

Growing up with immigrant parents was kind of shitty. Mom was always working or taking night classes, and Dad was working restaurant hours so he was never home during the evenings. I'll be honest, I didn't really get to know my mom and dad until my late teens even though we lived under the same roof. My parents were more like my roommates (except they were obligated to keep me alive).

When I look back at my childhood though, I think I got the perfect amount of neglect. My mom and dad worked their asses off to support my brother and I. But even though they worked a lot, they also spoiled us as much as they could with their limited time and money

My dad worked his way up from being a waiter to a general manager at the restaurant. My mom worked her way up from cleaning toilets and waitressing to finishing school, learning English, and then became a travel agent. Thanks to them I was fortunate enough to visit Vietnam at eight years old. That was pretty cool considering most kids don't get to travel overseas.

Then again, Vietnam was no Disneyland, especially in the 90's. In truth, my parents were literally paying money to travel back in time and live in poverty for four weeks. Some vacation!

Still, the fact that they could afford to do that had a lot to do with my aunts, uncles, grandmas and grandpas who took care of my brother and I when my parents were working.

When my mom dropped us off at someone's house we only had one rule: "Jo Lhec Jai." It's a Chinese phrase that means, "Be a good kid."

Because my mom used this phrase so often, it played a huge role in shaping me as a kid. The fact that I was surrounded by different people with whom I had to "be a good kid" around, made me a pretty good kid. I'd say "Hello" and "Goodbye," "Please" and "Thank you," and try my best to not be a brat. I also knew that if I fucked up I'd get a beating, so there was that fear factor as well. Over time, Jo Lhec Jai trickled down into all aspects of my life and helped me make good friends.

During our time of scarcity, there wasn't a lot of food at home, so my dad would do his best to bring some from the restaurant. However, since he worked late nights, we would eat dinner at 9:00 pm or whenever he got home. Leftovers would be lunch for my brother and I the next day. We never had breakfast.

When I started making friends in elementary school, being a good kid worked in my favour. I was likeable and I would trade lunches or even get snacks for free from the other kids. I played with them during recess and got invited to their birthday parties. Most of the kids I went to school with lived nearby. The more of them I hung out with at school, the more of them I got to hang out with after school. I'd get invited to their homes and we'd play Super Nintendo, jump on a trampoline, or run around outside. Normal kid stuff.

At some point I noticed that my friends had something I didn't have: a parent at home. That was normal to them. I wasn't envious or upset that my parents were working, but I realised that I must have been always looked hungry because the more I hung out with friends after school, the more food I was offered. My favourite phrase from my friend's parents was, "Would you like to stay over for supper"?

'Fuck yeah! I would *love* to stay over for supper!' was what went through my head. But since I was a good boy, I just said, "Yes, please."

This was the first time I can remember being aware of my environment and learning to adapt to it. Kids are clever; they figure out how to "cheat" the system. In my case, I discovered that if I was likeable, I got to have fun with friends, drink soda, and eat free food. I won the childhood lottery.

I now know this is a universal joy enjoyed by adults too. I mean, why do most people show up to a company Christmas party? Because it's free fun. You get liquored up, you eat all you want, and you don't pay for anything. It's a win, win, win.

I had so many friends that I planned my supper schedule around them. On Mondays I went to Chris's house, on Tuesdays it was Garret's, Wednesdays were at Brian's, Thursdays were at Steve's, and on Fridays I ate at Nik's. I saved my parents the trouble of feeding me through elementary school by being the kindest, most loving, and endearing mooch ever.

The trouble with having so many friends was that I started slacking in my schoolwork. Makes sense right? Wouldn't you rather hang out with your friends than do homework?

As a result, I was just a B-plus to C-minus student. I wasn't going to be a doctor or a lawyer. I didn't really get into trouble in class, but I never got recognized for anything either. I definitely walked the line though. I started hanging out with the "cool kids," who were also the troublemakers. I learned how to cheat on tests, and if I failed a quiz, I'd forge my mom's signature so it looked like she saw my grades (While I'm confessing to PG-13 delinquent shit, I also admit to stealing coins from my dad's coin jar to buy candy or Pokémon cards).

What I really want to acknowledge here though, is how much I learned from the people around me. Whether it was from watching my mom and dad work at the restaurant, struggling and building abundance; going to visit the Chinese temple and interacting with aunts, uncles, grandmas and grandpas there; or seeing my friends, their parents, and even the troublemakers at school, my upbringing gave me an amazing education.

Then something happened that changed my childhood. I discovered skateboarding.

My elementary school had one of those outdoor cement water parks where water would only flow during the summer. It had flower-themed Super Soakers and stationary water guns, a misting station, and a large wheelbarrow that would soak you with water.

This being Edmonton though, the most memorable thing about this water park was that for most of the year there was no water in it. As I walked home from school. I would see older kids skateboarding there. To me it was a massive concrete jungle. There was a large extended three stair, a ledge with a big drop at the end, and a cement wheelchair ramp that was the perfect height to grind on. The entire park had these perfect ledges that surrounded it. To me, it seemed like the greatest place on earth.

Watching these older kids throw themselves off obstacles or land a flip trick on a piece of wood with four wheels was the most awesome thing ever. They were fucking cool. I wanted to be them.

I remember begging my mom to buy me a skateboard. I didn't want anything else, just a skateboard. Predictably, when she finally got me one, it was of those $20 shitty no-name brands. Yet, I loved it and used that board until it broke.

For the first time in my life I was obsessed with something. I learned by watching, asking, and trying. And slowly, I started to get better and better. I would buy skateboarding magazines (using the money I stole from my dad) and read the articles over and over (Fun Fact: I still have those magazines. I must have a bit of 'Chinese hoarder blood' inside me).

Skateboarding was the perfect activity for me. I knew how financially limited my parents were at the time. I remember hearing them fight about money while my brother and I were in the next room playing Super Nintendo. Learning how to skateboard was cheap. The one barrier to entry was space, but if you could find a patch of cement, you could skateboard. Imagine being one of the few Chinese kids in a mostly-white elementary school learning how to skateboard at a waterpark with a bunch of pot-smoking, degenerate high schoolers. I loved it!

It was different from what the "normal" kids were doing. Skateboarding allowed me to run away from home without having to actually run away. It was the best thing that my environment gave to me and I took full advantage of it.

I started to hang out with those skateboarding kids every day and I learned important life lessons like how to set garbage cans on fire and egg cars. I never touched pot, but I did learn that smoking cigarettes was not my thing. One of those kids even gave me my first Playboy magazine and from it I learned to appreciate tits and ass.

Those were the glory days. Not a care in the world. We were just kids skateboarding and doing stupid shit with each other. That group of skateboarders, the community, was the best thing to ever happen to me. It was the best self-development tool for my upbringing and for my life.

Here's why.

Skateboarding is as real as it gets. I love how primitive the hierarchy is and the amount of skill it takes to be great at it. This is how I believe skateboarding directly bridges my career in sales and entrepreneurship.

You can't fake skill. The coolest skateboarders were the ones that were the best at the park. If you had no skill, you had no presence. Nobody cares if you had the nicest skateboard, clothes, or shoes. You would just be a poser. Skateboarding is all about the action and the tricks. You can't talk about skateboarding. Either you can do tricks or you can't. If I wanted to be the "cool" kid in skateboarding I needed to have skill. That is undeniable. Talk less, skate more.

Skateboarding taught me so many other things: being creative, having resiliency, being confident, consistency, failure, camaraderie, work ethic, problem solving, dreaming, goal setting, and visualization. It also taught me the value of skill, delayed gratification, and the ability to believe in myself.

I learned about consistency. Even if you land a trick once, you had to tell yourself, "I need to do it 10 out of 10 times." If you can't land the trick, you failed. Yet, the process of these little micro failures teaches you mental resiliency and the ability to delay your gratification until you can land it. The satisfaction you get when you finally land a trick that you have attempted 1000 times is amazing.

I received a sense of camaraderie with the other skateboarders because they wanted me to get better. They cheered me on when I attempted a crazy trick. They wanted me to set the bar higher and higher.

I got creative with skateboarding. I started looking at things differently. I started approaching obstacles or challenges with a different mindset. I dreamed and visualized how to land a trick. I set goals on what trick I wanted to achieve that week, that month or over the summer. I got coaching by the better skateboarders. It taught me to never give up. If I couldn't land a trick, I would literally attempt it every day until I did land it.

It taught me how to be fearless and courageous. If you're hucking yourself down a flight of stairs while attempting a kickflip you have to be a bit crazy, and truly believe in yourself.

It taught me to grow and get better. You spend countless hours and days just trying to land a trick that only gives you seconds of satisfaction. Most of all, skateboarding was fun and it continues to be fun.

Everything I've listed off about personal development is something you can read online or buy at the bookstore. You can even pay for a coach to tell you the same things. I didn't read about how to be a better skateboarder. I went out and I worked at it.

To use business as an example, you can't just read on how to start a business, you literally need to do it. There is no half-assing it. Either you start or you don't. Starting a business doesn't mean you need to have millions of dollars to open. It's executing the idea you have in your head. It's learning on a $20 skateboard, not waiting to get a $200 skateboard before you start.

It's the same as developing a new skill. You can't just think about what you want to be good at. Because you can either do something or you can't, just like you can either land a trick or you can't. To do anything you have to start, and keep working at it until you get it. Everything you do during the process will teach you about yourself, but you have to start somewhere.

Here's the fun part, you don't need to be famous, or the "cool kid" to execute you dreams, goals, or aspirations.

You just need to know that someone out there has done it before.

You don't need to know their name or where they are from. You just need to know that it's been done before and it's your turn to do it.

Like the satisfaction of landing your first kickflip, you can have the satisfaction of starting your first venture, learn how to play the guitar, start a vlog, learn a new language, or travel to a foreign country. How far you want to take it is completely up to you.

My environment taught me to be a good human being. Because if I wasn't a good kid, I didn't eat. But skateboarding honed in on the life skills that allowed my kindness to shine bright, which I eventually used for my career. Although this was the story about my upbringing, take a step back and dig deep into you own. What skills can you recognise that you earned and appreciated? Can you acknowledge the challenges you're facing and overcome them?

There is perspective in everything we do. I had to dig deep into my upbringing to identify who I am today. Just because I'm a 29-year-old "man-child" doesn't mean I should disown myself of a dream or aspiration. I may not be a pro skateboarder but the joy and fun of skateboarding as a kid transferred over to my businesses and my attitude towards life's obstacles. I look at the same problems you have but with my unique perspective.

Time to have fun and make some money.

Chapter One Summary

- Recognise that great Chinese food comes from the health inspector shutting down the restaurant not once but twice for being dirty, there's a really old-looking grandma watching over the children at the back corner table and you can't park in the parking lot.

- Bonus: if you do decide to park your vehicle in the parking lot, check your doors for dents and scratches and, if you are not of Chinese descent, expect that the moment you want someone to be held responsible for damages to your vehicle, it will just so happen that magically no-one in that restaurant will be able to speak English anymore.

- If you're a kind and good human being, you can mooch off people for a long time.

- Always attend your company Christmas party for the free booze, food, and fun. If the booze isn't free, always pre-drink.

- Go Skateboarding. Land a kickflip.

Chapter Two:

Humble-Bragging First World Problems

Going to high school is a huge transition for anyone and I was no different. In my district elementary school was grade 1 to 6, middle school was 7 to 9, and high school was 10 to 12. After that it was straight to university or college.

I went to high school with over 2,100 students and my graduating class was over 700 students. When I was registering for my courses I decided to take Chinese because I thought it would be an easy grade booster and a "free" class to dick around in. We also had the coolest teacher (shout out to Mr. Shao!). He was a Chinese immigrant to Canada himself and understood how hard it was to learn a language.

My brother and I had Chinese classes on Saturdays too, between 8:00 am and noon. My mom would force us to go no matter how much we cried or whined (seriously, if you ask a kid to wake up at 7 in the morning on a *Saturday* to go to school, you're gonna get push back, right?).

Once I was at the Chinese school and surrounded by other students I was okay. However, play was always on my mind so I barely did any work. There was this one time where I started drawing on my desk with an ink pen and everything I touched after that was blue. Another time I started poking holes in my desk. Literally, I would use anything sharp and just start digging in.

The teacher had to sit my mom down and tell her what I did. You might think she said I was always making a mess of things. Nope, my teacher did the complete opposite. She murdered my mom with kindness. She said that I was so intelligent that I didn't need to come to Chinese school anymore. She kicked me out because I was "too smart" and the classes were too easy for me. Because the class was not challenging enough, I would fuck around at my desk. That's why I got kicked out of one Chinese school.

I got kicked out of another Chinese school because I was caught cheating. I would come into class and the teacher would tell us to put everything away for a test. I had no idea we had a test so I turned around and copied some other kid's work. I didn't get away with it, but so what? It meant I didn't have to go to school the next weekend. Score!

When I look back, I wish I hadn't been such a shitty student because I wouldn't have gotten kicked out of Chinese school. Now I can only speak elementary grade Chinese that is very harsh and "redneck" sounding. As a Chinese kid born in Canada, I kind of knew my native language, but if you actually tried to talk to me in Mandarin I would have given you a blank stare. Back then my peers were way better than me so I made up for it the way I knew best. By cheating.

When you're a kid you just want to have fun and you don't know shit about responsibility. You just move on to the next adventure. I totally see now how much of a brat I was for my mom because those classes cost her time and money.

During those years I saw both of my parents' companies grow. After my mom worked her way up the corporate ladder in the travel agency world she started her own travel company specializing in south-east Asian tours, mostly to China, Hong Kong, and Vietnam.

Since our high school was one of the biggest in the district they would get a lot of funding for trips. When I was in Grade 11 there were two trips for students to go on: one to Europe and the other to China. When my Chinese teacher was organizing the trip to China, he asked us students if we knew a travel agent. Of course I put my hand up.

"My mom is a travel agent!" I said.

That was the first time I gave my mom a referral for her business and that school trip ended up getting my mom many years of high school and middle school business because the other Chinese teachers and schools started using her services.

When it was announced that the trip to China was a go and students were allowed to sign up, a lot of my classmates started to ask if I was going to go. I said, "Sure. If you go, I'll go."

That trip was a blast. For two weeks I got to hang out with my friends in a different country, stay in hotels with the cute girls in class, sit beside them on the bus and sneak out of my hotel room at night to hang with them until late in the morning. That's what a high school trip is all about: getting crazy with your homies and making memories (Hey, I even made out in bed with one of the girls. Nothing really happened though since I was young and too dumb to know how to use my boner. So I just tucked it away when we were kissing. Oh, those good ol' frigate days.).

As my mom was finding success with her travel business, she started asking my dad to go to China to do groundwork there for her while his business partner watched their restaurant. Since my mom got involved in the school trip to China because of me, it made sense that my dad should come along on it.

It was awesome because I shared a room with my dad and he didn't care when I came back because he knew I was with my school friends. I was spoiled. I didn't have to do anything to get on that trip.

“Mom, I want to go to China," was all I said.

“Okay," she replied, and without another word my parents did everything: applied for my visa, made the booking, and paid for it all.

I had the kind of parents that valued travelling. Anywhere in the world I wanted to go, they would pay for. By the time I graduated high school I’d been back and forth to Asia half a dozen times. I thought this was normal. I thought everyone had the ability to just hop on a plane and fuck off to another country.

Boy, was I wrong about that...

My reality check came after high school. I was extremely spoiled and I didn’t even know it. My mom did though. She knew I needed to come down to Earth, so she decided to kick me out of the house and send me to Vietnam.

"I don't want to go to Vietnam *again*."

It was the word, "again," that triggered my mom.

You, like her, might be thinking, "Wow, Wilson, you got a chance to go to Asia for another free holiday.”

Yes, but this time my mom decided it was going to be different.

A few months later I was on a flight to Vietnam. No Canadian summer for me. No hanging with my friends. I was going to live in Viet-fucking-nam for the next four months. Not only that, but there would be no fancy hotel with air conditioning and a breakfast buffet. I was going by myself to live with my mom’s side of the family, and they were poor. Like, extreme poverty poor. Their home had no sealed doors, windows, or rooms. It was open concept living for people, bugs, wind, dirt, and smells.

This was my first taste of independence. I was experiencing the world for the first time by myself. It was uncomfortable and challenging. Yet going on tours with my dad and watching him work had rubbed off on me, so I wasn't a complete idiot when it came to travelling. I made it to the right gate, boarded my flight, and 14 hours later I was in Vietnam.

I don't remember much about that flight except that there were in-flight movies and unlimited ice cream. I do remember what it was like in Vietnam when I arrived, though. Pouring.

Despite the rain, most of my aunts, uncles and cousins came to pick me up from the airport. With them came the predictable comments.

"You're so handsome."

"You've grown so tall and big."

"Do you have a girlfriend yet?"

If you reply, "No, I don't have a girlfriend," you are bound to get, "Why not?" On the other hand, if you answer, "Yes," the next question is, "So, when are you getting married?" (Skipping ahead, once you are married, it's, "When are you going to have kids?")

Being a high school kid in Canada without a girlfriend is pretty standard. But when you live in poverty you should be married and the family breadwinner at 17. If you're lucky, like my parents, you'll live long enough to see your kids grow up. My dad was one of eight children. I reckon my grandparents just popped them out, crossed their fingers, and relied on survival of the fittest.

Adjusting to Vietnam's climate was challenging. Canada was cool and dry, Vietnam was hot and humid. I hated the fact that I would sweat all the time. No matter how many times I showered, my body felt sticky. Still, it wasn't really showering – it was just pouring a bucket of rainwater collected the day before over your head. There was no such thing as hot water, or warm water for that matter. To have a hot shower we had to boil water on the stove and then bring it into the showering room.

The shower "stall" was just a tiny aged cement room with large cracks in the wall that gave you a great view of the living room (and presumably gave anyone in the living room a great view of you). The shower water exited through the house's drainage system. There was nothing as fancy as a pipe, just a trough that guided the dirty water out into the street. This was Vietnamese hygiene at its most basic.

Another way to shower was outside during a tropical storm. I remember the kids around the neighbourhood taking off their clothes in the streets and showering under the runoff from the roof of a shack. Taking a shower outside was one way those kids found fun in the face of poverty.

Rainstorms were also when street cleaning happened. Since garbage disposal in Vietnam is something that, like Christmas, happens once a year, there is always leftover food and trash on the sidewalks and streets. Getting rid of your garbage in Vietnam is easy: drop it behind you and walk away. This was great for the street rats – buffet meals daily.

Rats and rain are the two main ways that people dispose of their garbage in Vietnam. A rainstorm washes away dirt, grime, and animal poop, of which there is plenty. In Canada it's just common courtesy to pick up your dog's shit. In Vietnam, the rain does it for you.

During a downpour is also when critters come indoors to find shelter. At night that really sucks. I'd try to take a piss and I'd see these beady rat eyes glowing back at me in the dark. Since rats literally eat everything they grow to unfathomable sizes. I kid you not, the rats I saw were the size of a small kitten or Chihuahua dog. It was fucking disgusting.

This is the stuff my extended family had to deal with on a day-to-day basis. I eventually got over it, but only because I would talk to myself while walking down the stairs, asking the rats and roaches to leave me alone during my time of vulnerability.

But rats and roaches weren't the only things I had to worry about.

Now let me just say, I'm not really scared of spiders because the ones we have in Canada are the size of a coin and eat annoying flies and mosquitoes. But in Vietnam, they're massive!

On one particular warm and humid afternoon I needed to poop real bad. Should be no biggie. So, I go to the back of the house and head over to the washroom. I drop my pants and proceed to drop the kids off at the pool. Then it was time to wipe.

But I couldn't.

The loaf of toilet paper was on my right-hand side, but I couldn't get to it because there was a massive fucking spider the size of a dinner plate inside the toilet paper dispenser. Trust me, when you're faced with a creature bigger than your hand while you're taking a shit, something funny happens to you. You start negotiating. Our negotiations went something like this:

I said, "Um, excuse me, I'm trying to wipe my ass. Could you just, like, move to the right a little so I could grab some toilet paper?"

But the spider didn't respond and didn't move.

"Come on, man, don't make me walk out with crumbs on my butt. That's not cool. You're not being nice at all. "

Still nothing.

I begged. "Please, dude, don't make me yell for my aunt. Come on, please!"

No response.

There was nothing for it.

"AUNTIE!!! I NEED TOILET PAPER."

Hearing that, my aunt rushed over to the door and started talking me through it.

"Why you need toilet paper? There should be some in there."

"There's a spider on the toilet paper," I replied desperately.

"Oh, *that's* all? Just kill it?" she responded, as though killing mammoth-sized tropical spiders was a normal thing.

'Don't worry, Wilson,' I thought. 'Sure, go ahead and kill the spider that's big enough to eat you and your cat. No biggie.'

But I couldn't. Instead, I shamelessly flushed and walked right out of there. The spider won and I had to go rinse off my butt in the shower room!

[Fun fact: I'm a little crazy now because anytime I encounter a spider I won't try to harm it. I just ask it to kindly leave.]

So, I've talked about two aspects of Vietnamese life that begin with 's': showering and shitting. Here's a third.

Sleep.

If you're thinking mattress on a bare wooden floor, bingo, you got it! And not only was it a mattress on the floor, it was in a communal sleeping room, meaning four or five people sleeping on the floor around each other. Since I was a guest, I at least got the good mattress. My aunt and cousins would rotate where they slept each night so everyone got equal use of the only mosquito net in the house.

Sleeping on the floor on top of a mattress isn't too bad. After a few weeks you get used to the back pain. Even though Vietnam has tropical temperatures, nighttime can be cold. Not like Canada-cold where it's dry and you can just layer up. Vietnam cold is wet and it chills you down to the bone.

After a rainstorm, that wet-cold feeling comes around and you need to sleep with a blanket. Thankfully, I had the necessities: a pillow, a blanket and a mattress. The other thing that made me feel at ease was the music from my mp3 player. Now, this was way before streaming or phones that could hold an entire music library, this was a 256 MB mp3 player (yes, that's megabytes, not gigabytes). I couldn't even charge it with a USB cord, I had to use AAA batteries to keep it running.

What was great about the limited space was that I had to choose my 40 favourite songs. There was no room for error. Those would be the only 40 songs I could play, so I had to choose the perfect mix.

Trust me, being in a foreign country with no friends, speaking a language your relatives can barely understand, and playing with the younger kids around the neighbourhood because there's nothing better to do gets old pretty quick. So my music was my home-away-from-home, it saved me from extreme boredom. I brought my mp3 player everywhere just in case I needed a pick-me-up from whatever I was experiencing. Most of those wet, cold nights I would have my earphones in and listen to whatever until I fell asleep.

One particular night, when it was pouring so hard that the rain splashing off the tin roof echoed through the house, I put in my earphones and tried to drift off. As the rain banged on the roof, I would occasionally hear the sky rumble with thunder, or someone in the room snoring. I was a light sleeper, so as I tossed and turned, trying to find a good position, my one earphone would pop out. Half asleep, I'd lazily find it with my eyes closed and fumble it back into my ear. Then I would toss and turn and it would fall out again.

Eventually, tired of this, I decided to sleep on my back. I shifted and moved and finally found a comfy spot on my back. Earphones in, I felt locked and loaded for a good night's sleep. Then, as I was finally on the verge of falling asleep, my earphone fell out again on my cheek.

Wait a minute… It couldn't have... I was sleeping on my back and still heard music playing in both ears. At this point I went from fast asleep to fear. What the fuck was on my face? I was petrified. I started to panic, but I didn't dare move. All I could think of was, 'Holy shit, what's on my face? Get the fuck off my face!' (I'm getting goosebumps down my arm and spine just typing this story out.) I felt another tickle and I smacked whatever it was into oblivion. I ripped the blanket off my body, got up quickly, and looked down to inspect whatever it was.

Cockroaches.

Not just one tiny roach. There were dozens of them. Godzilla-sized roaches were sleeping with me. They were hugging my body, stealing my heat, using me to keep warm. I screamed and shook them all off my mattress and they scattered into the dark in all directions.

I remember being just mad. I was disgusted, upset, and fuming that I was sleeping with roaches.

My aunt woke up beside me and asked what happened.

"I was *sleeping with roaches*!" I said.

I shit you not, my aunt just started laughing and asked me, "What do you want to do about it?"

Welcome to Vietnam.

It was at that moment that I knew there was nothing I could do about my circumstances. I learned how to accept poverty and I understood that this was how my aunts and uncles lived every day, and that my mom and dad used to live like this too. That was the moment at which this trip became truly humbling.

After a few more months in Vietnam I finally got the chance to have a *real* vacation before I went back home to Canada. I was going to fly to Hong Kong to meet my dad, who was going to take me around Hong Kong and China. Though I was just excited because I loved tennis and wanted to buy a ton of cheap tennis clothes.

But as I said goodbye to my aunts and uncles at the airport in Vietnam, I sensed they knew I had changed. I was no longer fussy about what I ate, I could sleep almost anywhere, and the biggest change of all was that I had stopped complaining.

I enjoyed the trip to Hong Kong with my dad, and I got a bunch of tennis gear (I have photos of me wearing this green and white polo shirt and shorts, and others of me in an all-white outfit with navy blue accents. That was my favourite late-teen fashion: tennis wear), but after I came back home, my mom never asked me about that trip. I thought it was weird since she was the one who sent me on it. But let's be honest, she knew what I needed to go through.

I went to Vietnam from a privileged country just for one summer and it made me realize that my life in Canada wasn't that bad. The living conditions in Vietnam were awful and my relatives had to live in them every day. Living it made me realise why my parents sent money back to my relatives. It was to increase the quality of life for my parents' brothers and sisters. I realized that my mom sent me on the trip not to punish me, but to humble me. Sure, living in poverty for a few weeks wouldn't do the trick on its own, but now, when I look back at my experience in Vietnam, that whole summer makes a lot of sense.

After living this experience at 17 years old, I knew that if there were any challenges ahead in my future, I would be okay. I didn't have to live in poverty anymore. I didn't have to sleep with the roaches or negotiate with spiders. I didn't have to shower with a bucket or collect rainwater. This is how I got a chance to humble-brag my first world problems.

Chapter Two Summary

- If you suck at a second language, you can cheat your way to getting high marks.

- Remember that rules at home do not apply for international school trips. Seek fun. Always.

- Never talk back to your mom or else she will send you Vietnam or beat you, whichever is cheaper.

- Remember that taking off your clothes in public to shower in the rain may be prohibited in your area. But I think you should try it. Let me know how it goes.

- By sleeping with roaches you automatically become the bug whisperer. You might even make a new friend while taking a shit.

Chapter Three:

Fun Hours Equals Fun Money

After I graduated from high school I didn't know what I wanted to do. I thought I would just get a job and work. Most of my friends said they were going to take a year off, work for a while and then go back to school. I told my mom what my friends were doing and she was opposed to it. I honestly thought that making money would be something she would be okay with me doing. Instead she used logic and gave me advice that I share with everyone today.

"It doesn't matter how long you take to finish school, just go to school," she said. "What is another four years of school? If you want to work, you have another 40 years to work. Go to school now."

So I had to go to university, no matter what. I had no other options. I didn't disagree with her, I just told her I don't know what I wanted to take. For her it didn't matter, as long as I was in school.

It was 2008 and there were many schools to choose from. I decided to apply only to one, the one that my mom went to. I got in too. Funnily enough, my saving grace was my one elective in high school, which had boosted my mark enough to get me accepted. Can you guess what course that was?

Yes, it was Chinese. The thing I had sucked at most was my ticket to university.

In my first semester at university I didn't make any friends, but around October I got a girlfriend. I'd already been talking to her on-and-off for about a year during high school, but it hadn't started too well. We first met at a house party and she didn't like me at all. I hated this, so I did what I did best – I won her over, got her phone number, and we became friends. After that we would chat using MSN Messenger or Nexopia and talk on the phone almost every day. On weekends we literally spent hours talking. I had to use multiple cordless home-phones because our calls outlasted the batteries.

In the first year of knowing this girl we must have hung out together only three times. All we did was talk on the phone. I liked her though. It was like something out of an eHarmony commercial. But I didn't force anything, I just took it slow.

Just before her birthday she got her driver’s license and a car. I was ecstatic. It was only then that I confessed that I liked her. After that we officially started “seeing each other.” That was October 2008.

My girlfriend was at the university a couple of train stations away from mine. She would visit me from time to time and introduce me to some of her old high school classmates who went to my university. I did the rest and made new friends.

So university had started off pretty well. I was in academia, I had a girlfriend, and I was making new connections. I was your average student, and by April 2008 I was studying for finals and preparing for the summer break. To be honest though, I sucked at studying with other people. I used school more as a social club. I would mostly sit in the cafeteria shooting the shit with my buddy, talking about life. That was my idea of studying. Though one evening my mom asked me what I wanted to do for summer work. I had no idea.

On one of those shit shooting sessions my buddy saw this big blue poster that said “Summer Work” and told me to try it out. It had those little phone number tabs at the bottom so I ripped one off and made the call.

The company was scheduling interviews that evening so I took the latest slot, which was at 6:00 pm. It was about 4:00 pm at the time so I had two hours to head to their office. My buddy and I didn't drive, I hated taking the bus, and my parents were working overseas so I called my aunt. I sold her on the idea of me getting a summer job, then I stressed that the interview was tonight and that I needed a ride. What loving aunt wouldn't help her nephew in those circumstances?

She came right away, picked me up from school, and drove me 10 minutes to the address I was given. The building was pretty shady-looking, so I told my aunt to wait until I made sure it was the right place, then I went up the flight of stairs and into a bright white room. A man came out of an office and advised me that it would be a group interview and it could take about 90 minutes. That was fine with me. It was better than studying. I ran back downstairs to tell my aunt and she said she'd pick me up when I was done.

To cut a long story short, I went through the interview process, the pre-screening, the product demonstration, and the post-interview chit-chat and I got the job. I was so excited. I called my aunt and told her I was ready.

When she finally arrived and I hopped into the car she asked me, "What will you be doing?"

"I'll sell knives," I replied.

"You'll do what?" she asked as if she thought I was joking.

"I'll sell knives," I repeated.

"Oh, I don't think your mom is going to like that."

"What's not to like? She wanted me to get a job and I got one, first try."

When my mom finally got home from her tour I told her I would need the car for the last weekend of April.

"What for?" she asked.

"I've got training for a job," I told her. I wanted to surprise her with the news so I had a dumbass smirk on my face.

"What's the training for? What do you do?"

"I sell knives," I said.

"You do what?"

"I sell knives."

My mom then proceeded to tell me all the reasons why I shouldn't do it. It took what seemed like forever to convince her that I knew what I was doing (which I didn't – I just thought it would be exciting to try something new). But I believe that if you're stubborn and you care enough, eventually people will back down, so I was relentless. In the end my mom told me I should try it out and she would help me.

Many times before I had asked friends and family for their advice or opinion, but on that day I realised that if I really wanted to do something, I should do it no matter what. I know this way of thinking can bite you in the ass, but so far it has served me well.

After my exams were finished I had a few days to myself before the big training day. Then I went back to that shady-looking office and prepared myself for 24 hours of learning. Who would have thought I would be excited to learn again right after studying for my exams?

For the training sessions I wore my high school graduation suit, which, let me tell you, did not fit well. Actually, it was my dad's suit, and he's 5-foot-1, a full 8 inches shorter than me. My ankles were breezy for those three days.

You might be wondering why I was suited up and learning how to sell knives, who I would be selling them to, and how much I was going to get paid. Well, here's the short version.

I was an 18-year-old university student going home-to-home selling knives. It was a commission-based job with base pay per appointment. I sold through referrals. If it was your son, you might be extremely skeptical. I was jumping for joy though. This was my first "real" job. I'd hated serving at the restaurant, though that was pretty much child labour.

My only previous exposure to in-home selling was as a child watching a Kirby vacuum cleaner salesman. Kirby was the cream of the crop in the market in the 90's. Their vacuum cleaners cost around $2,000. The sales rep would come in and pretty much vacuum the whole house, show off the custom attachments, and then leave behind a free gift when my parents didn't buy anything. Like most people, my mom and dad didn't have $2,000 sitting around to spend on a vacuum cleaner.

After the three days of training I was ready to launch into door-to-door sales myself, starting with two of my aunts and the parents of two of my high school friends. I was going out in the real world with a blue bag full of knives ready to sling some blades.

My first appointment was with the aunt who drove me to my interview. It was supposed to take around 45 minutes, but she couldn't sit through my shitty translation of English to Chinese so she just took my catalogue, flipped through it, and ordered $100 worth.

'Great!' I thought, 'I've got my first sell out of the way. I'm 1-for-1.'

I still had three more appointments, but I had a really great feeling about this gig.

From my aunt's I walked to my high school friend's place for my next appointment, unaware that my naivety was going to slap me across the face.

In training we were taught how awesome the knives were and how to deal with rejection. But they didn't really teach us how to deal with difficult customers. At my next appointment, the mom was pretty neutral, but the dad would bring out his knives and explain why they were so much better than mine. I wasn't happy that someone was shitting on the knives I was trying to sell!

That appointment was awful, but at least it meant I got my first "no sale" out of the way early. I was 1-for-2 and still had two more appointments to go.

But by the end of that day I had one sale and three back-to-back no-sales in a row. That's a success ratio of 25%. It didn't bother me too much though because I had no idea what my employer's sales standard were. But after the weekend I found out that I had the worst sales return in my group.

On Monday we handed in our orders. Other reps in my class brought in sales worth thousands of dollars. I brought in a measly $100. Then and there I started to learn that there is a hierarchy in sales: the more you sell, the more prestige and recognition you get. If you don't sell, you get nothing.

Thankfully, after advance training, I started to get better, and after 10 days I sold $4,000. I was really proud of myself, especially when I got two commission promotions. I was having fun and really enjoying the job. The only downside was when I had to show my mom how much I made in ten days. At $437.80, it was underwhelming, but it was something.

Once again I was earning child labour wages. But the big difference was that I was actually enjoying myself. I kept telling my mom that I was learning a lot and that I wanted to keep going. I told her that it didn't matter how much I was working. I was earning money not asking for it. That was really rewarding for me.

Soon I started getting referrals that were too far for me to take the bus, so I would ask my aunt or parents to drive my ass around. I knew they would get tired of that, so I eventually asked my parents to let me use the car. I had to agree to their conditions: they got first priority, I could only use it on weekends and weekday evenings, and only after they finished their errands. But it worked. My travelling salesmen job had landed me a vehicle.

Now let's digress and talk about Asian drivers.

There are two types of Asian drivers. The first is slow as fuck, methodical, going 50 in a 60 zone, triple shoulder-checking, and ultra-safe. This is the kind of driver where you're like, "Holy shit, drive faster!" But these are also the ones who drive on the right-hand side of the road and let you pass, so they aren't the worst Asian drivers. In this group it is either a middle-aged Asian woman in some sort of SUV, or a really old Asian man in a 1998 Toyota Corolla. He's often also bald, wearing thick turtle glasses, leaning forward, and squinting at the road ahead of him. You can usually pick these men out through the window because they are wearing the universal old man Asian uniform: the fleece sweater vest.

The second type of Asian driver is the "need for speed, heat-bag" Asian. These overconfident drivers are usually in their 20s, have some sort of koi fish, dragon or tiger tattoo, and one of two hair options: 1) spiky anime hair, or 2) bald as can be. You can usually pick them out because they are all-tricked-out tuner car guys. These guys always have some sort of project car in their driveway that gets a sun tan and collects rust. They also currently have, or have had, a Toyota Supra. Last but not least, their car has an exhaust that you can hear a mile away. (Bonus judgement: this one either is, or at one time was, a drug dealer.) I prefer this type of driver because they have cool-looking cars and they usually speed. They are great for the highways because they are the rabbits for the cops.

I was neither slow nor fast. I was the strategic driver. I guess that makes three types of drivers (let's be real, everyone thinks they drive amazingly). Since there is less traffic in the summer due to people leaving the city for their holidays, I would plan my trips during non-rush hour times and never leave the house between 4:00 pm and 6:00 pm because the people I booked my appointments with would be driving back home. So I did all my appointments either in the afternoons with the housewives, or after 7:00 pm when I got to sit down with both the husband and wife.

As I progressed up the commission ladder, something magical happened. I began to make more money with putting in less time, effort, and energy. This was incredible! But it was also a double-edged sword for the 18-year-old me.

I had it good. I was living at home. Mom and Dad did the grocery shopping. I made enough money for gas and going out with my friends. And really, that's all I needed. When I was motivated, I'd sell and make money. But once I'd made enough to meet my immediate needs, I didn't sell anything. I got complacent.

Our sales office had weekly team meetings and every week there would be a sales rep who would continue to sell consistently, get the money, and get recognition. Back then I didn't know if I enjoyed being around high achievers. Either I would get envious of their achievements, or I would get inspired to keep working hard. Because I wanted to be a top rep, selling lots and making shitloads of money. But I did not want to work hard. So I mostly felt envy. I was a below-average sales rep, with a below-average work ethic and an above-average dream.

I just wanted to have fun. And that's when it hit me, I was looking at work all wrong. It wasn't some thing where you exchange effort for money. Every appointment I went on was an opportunity to have fun. I didn't care if I got a sale, I just wanted to have a good time. The crazy thing is, the more fun I had, the more sales I got. And when I looked at the top sales reps, I realized that they were having fun too.

Today I love high achievers. They make me want to work harder and inspire others. To me, the bottom line is that if you want to make fun money, you have to put in fun hours.

How do you do that?

There's nothing worse than making money for the sake of making money. Sure, this can get you a huge pile of money, but you haven't used it to gain experience or accomplish your goals or dreams. Life happens, and you definitely need to make sure your main bills are paid on time. However, you should also make it a goal to spend the money you've earned.

You can delay gratification by working two or three jobs, putting in overtime or having a side hustle. There's nothing wrong with that if you're investing your time and money with the intent to have fun later. You can also embrace the challenges and stomach the failures of entrepreneurship. It isn't usually glamorous, but it is fun, and that's what I'm talking about here.

Whatever you do, I suggest working towards an experience goal or something you want to buy. These are easier goals to achieve. Maybe you want to save enough money to go to a music festival in Europe. Or perhaps you're aiming to buy your first guitar. Do the napkin math and see how many hours you need to put in to get whatever it is you really want.

I had many different adventures in entrepreneurship in university. One of those adventures involved learning about penny stocks. I would go on forums to learn about the next new thing then put in a few hundred dollars and earn a few hundred. It gave me a crazy high. I'd set my alarm for 7:00 am so I could buy and sell shares when the markets opened at 7:30 am. I would dream about winning the penny stock lottery. But reality wasn't so kind and I lost it all. It was still a great learning experience though, and fun while it lasted.

Later in life a friend and I tried to sell Pokémon Go T-shirts. We spent about $1,000 on stock and sold maybe a few dozen. We definitely didn't get our money's worth and most of those shirts are still in his basement.

Instead of spending so much time and energy researching stocks or figuring out how to sell T-shirts, I could have had a normal part-time job and bought stupid shit with my wages. But that would have been boring. Instead, I invested my money on things that produced absolutely no monetary return, but rewarded me with experience. I learned that losing money isn't fun, but being able to fabricate an idea and execute on it because you decided to is important for developing your mindset.

There is no one way to make fun hours equal fun money. Whatever you're doing, as long as it's fun, challenging, and promoting personal growth, the monetary gains will follow soon after you've developed the skills necessary to execute on your ideas.

This is where I see friends, family, and many other people doing it wrong: they are chasing the money but not having fun doing it.

Say you were great with numbers in high school and you decided to become an accountant. You go, crush out school, get your degree, and get that job. The years pass by and you have money in the bank, you have the house, the car, the toys. Yet you're miserable. You're stuck. You can't quit your job because you're paying for all the shit you bought thinking it was going to bring you happiness.

Or maybe you're a free bird. Whenever money or opportunity is presented you take it. You have fun all the time. You travel, buy things, go places, and when you're back home, you work whatever job you need to so you can chase that fun again. But you see your friends start a family, grow their careers, buy toys and houses, and you're envious because you don't have money to do that.

Either way, what matters is how you decide to live your life when you finally acknowledge your own unhappiness. That is when you need to make the executive decision to change, because no one else will do it for you, regardless of who is in your life.

My goal in this chapter is to help you empathize with yourself. To understand what you want, how you can make the money to pay for it, and have fun at the same time.

If you're that rare breed of person who knew exactly what they wanted to do when they grew up, congratulations! Go live your life. If you're like me, however, and have adult ADHD, where you just want to see where life takes you, then you need a plan or strategy to win at the game of life.

Maybe you're in school and the pressure is on to choose a major that will get you a great career. You need to ask yourself what it is you really want. Are you working towards a job that will make you a lot of money but hating what you have to do to get there? If so, you're going to be that guy or gal who is stuck in a career they hate, making money they don't need, and losing precious time that could be used to pursue something actually enjoyable.

If that sounds like you, it's time to talk to your ego. Are you willing to take a pay cut? Can you give up materialistic things to work on something you really love? Maybe its fitness, cars, beauty, fashion, vlogging, travelling, sports, animals. It doesn't matter. What does matter is that you can work towards that thing you want. And if you just google it, you'll see that someone out there has already paved the way for you.

What if I told you that by putting your extra time into your passion project, one day you'll make the same salary you're making now but you'll be following your dreams? Would you do it?

I hope you'd say, "Yes, I want that!"

Keep your options open. Keep working at your main gig, but plug away at your "fun" stuff every day too. If you're willing to put extra effort into whatever it is you spend your fun hours on, sooner or later it will pay off in fun money. Sure, it can sometimes take years before that fun money starts coming in, but once you start seeing the first small tangible results coming in, you won't even think about all those extra hours you put in to your passion. You will have built something that you wanted to, and you had fun doing it!

This book is an example of that. I decided to write it because it was on the list of dream projects that I wrote down many years ago.

"Wouldn't it be funny if I was an author?" asked the guy whose girlfriend had to rewrite his papers for him because they were so awful.

What better way to have fun than to write a book in 120 days, I decided. And since you're reading this, it means I finished the book and became a self-published author.

Maybe I'll make money off this book and maybe I won't. Either way, I had a lot of fun writing it and surprising people who didn't think I could. Whatever I make will be fun money from putting in fun hours. It might not be really profitable, but to me it will be worth every hour spent doing it.

I have a friend who has worked in the corporate banking industry for years. She loves building LEGO, she literally has thousands of dollars worth. She also loves going to barre classes.

What does this have to do with fun money and fun hours?

My friend's barre class was shutting down due to unforeseen circumstances and she was sad that her fun was coming to an end. What better way to have fun than to start her own barre class, she thought. She found a core group of people, had some drama here and there, went through her challenges, then almost a year later she partnered up with a yoga studio. She is now getting advance payments and more and more people are signing up for her classes. As a result, she gets to do barre for free and she is learning about running a business. Plus any extra money she makes can go towards more LEGO.

When you're having fun, you'll never do it for the money. However, if you're intelligent about it, you can definitely make money doing the things you love. Go and figure out what you enjoy doing and find a way to monetize it.

Is that making videos, vlogs, or writing blogs about it? Is it by selling something in an unconventional way? Do you need to find like-minded people with skill sets that would help you? Figure that shit out, because it really is fun when your dream starts coming true. So go out there and put in fun hours to make fun money.

Chapter Three Summary

- If you want to borrow your parents' car, get a sales job.
- Always double check to see if the person driving slowly is an Asian driver or not.
- Remember to save your grad clothes because one day your son or daughter will wear them.
- Don't do it for the money. Do it because you love it.
- As a reminder, there is a delay in the monetary gains when you're first starting out your fun.

Chapter Four:

Calculated Fun

There were many highs and lows when I worked at my first sales job. I was still very young and unsure about my ability as a salesman. Nonetheless, I kept plugging away at it. Then, during a "What am I doing with my life?" phase, I decided to try for a part-time job at a skateboard shop. My friend was the manager and he told me that if I applied I would get the job.

This was my first encounter with the idea that it's not what you know but who you know. I loved skateboarding and I knew how to sell stuff, yet it was knowing the right person that allowed me to skip the line of applicants. Sure, the work was just stocking shelves and folding clothes, but it showed me that knowing the right person can make it much easier to get the things you want.

After working a year at the skate shop and having plugged away at my knife-selling job for two years, an opportunity for advancement came along. The knife company wanted to train me to become a branch manager. It would be an eight-month training program from September until April and then I would have to move away from home to run the business in a different city until the end of August.

I couldn't fathom how big an opportunity it really was, but I thought it would be fun to try it out. Because when a company offers you a position in management it is truly intriguing.

I wanted success. I wanted fun. I wanted something significant in my life. I was a nobody in the knife-selling business and I wanted to be somebody for someone. I wanted to feel what I thought the top sales reps I looked up to felt. I was fun and silly and I enjoyed being around my colleagues, but I was a lurker, a lingerer. I didn't really do much except go to meetings and make friends. I watched other people get better and succeed while I was left in the dust thinking, 'Oh, that's okay. I'll get there too, sooner or later.'

I didn't know if I was ready for it though. It had taken me 21 months just to get the final sales promotion to the highest level of commission, that's the same promotion most people get between four months and a year. Still, I was excited because I had become part of the company norm and that was where the real fun and challenge begins. That's where the elite get to compete.

A sales job is always a competition. There is always someone better than you, and when you think you've reached the summit, you find there is another beast higher than you on the food chain. The pursuit of success, abundance, and recognition is infinite. But I knew I was on the right path.

All the other branch manager candidates from across the country and I were flown to Toronto for a weekend to kick off our training at a hotel across from Niagara Falls. We got wined and dined and rubbed elbows with the best managers in the company. I was spoiled. I still wasn't really that good at the job, but my manager at the time wanted me to be a part of the sales empire he was building, and I was excited to have a chance at bat.

Young and impressionable, I went through the rest of the sales training and programs back home. I was taught how to hire, train, and recruit. I learned systems for marketing. I learned how to negotiate a lease. I learned how to barter products for services and even trade services. I learned how to talk with universities and colleges to give students the same opportunity I received.

After my training was done I had to make an executive decision: do I move away and become the manager of an office all by myself, or stay at home and continue to work in the local office? I had to weigh the pros and cons and the risk I was about to take on. If I decided to leave home and start this crazy business, the worst case scenario was that I would lose four months of my summer, I wouldn't get to hang out with my friends, I'd lose money, I'd have failed at the business, and I would still feel insignificant. The best case scenario was that I would find success and abundance (although I had no idea what that even looked like). My pride and ego were on the line.

I knew what mediocrity looked like, I had lived it for almost two years. I was tired of being lame, and I didn't want to quit while I was at the bottom. Many people give up when things are tough and hard because it gives them an excuse to say, "Fuck it!" and leave. I didn't want to be like that. It had also been two years of encouragement and belief. Sometimes when you lack belief in yourself, the right encouragement can shift your mentality from "I can't" to "I can." Not once did my company put me down, or tell me I couldn't succeed. They always told me I could.

Starting a business is really scary though. Not only do you have to put your money where your mouth is, everyone around you is watching you do it. Some of them will want you to find success, some will want you to fail and some don't want you to try because they don't want to see you fail (which is kind of like saying they don't think you can do it, but in a nice way).

I honestly had no idea what the journey was going to be like, but I said yes to being a manager, and it was the best thing I could have done for myself. It didn't matter what my friends thought, my parents wanted, or anyone else believed. This was my chapter. I wanted to write it and I didn't need anyone telling me what I could or couldn't do. It was that simple.

During finals week I studied, played video games for escapism, and looked online to search for a place to rent for four months in the city I was moving to, Grande Prairie, Alberta. I soon learned that most landlords didn't want to rent on those terms because I wasn't offering long-term income. Either that or they would charge a ridiculous amount to make up for the fact that I would only be there for four months. After my experience in Vietnam though, I didn't care where I stayed as long as I had a roof over my head.

Since I was a student, I figured I might be able to stay at the school. There was only one college in the city and I found out that they offered room and board to students for ultra-cheap. I jumped at that. And while I was living there, I found it funny that during the day I was a branch manager and young professional, but at night I was a just another 20-year-old kid trying to do laundry and grocery shop.

My favourite part about moving out was that I could finally eat what I wanted without my very-Chinese mom telling me that everything I ate was unhealthy. One of the first things I bought was a 4-litre jug of chocolate milk and a block of marble cheese. We never ate dairy products at home so I was making up for that. Yep, I moved out of my parents' house to start a business and stock up my fridge with chocolate milk and cheese.

Once I was officially settled at the college dorm, with food in the fridge and a 24-pack of toilet paper ("What do you mean the rental doesn't come with toilet paper?"), I was ready to be a young professional and get my office set up.

My office was conveniently located in downtown Grande Prairie. It was a small room in a large open space on the second floor of a brown brick building. I set up my tables and chairs and made sure to put those tacky business posters on the walls, the ones that say inspirational things like "SUCCESS" above a picture of something irrelevant like a lighthouse overlooking the ocean.

A friend of mine was doing his work placement in the city and I asked him if he wanted to help out. He took some cringe-worthy photos of me and we celebrated my success by accidentally locking ourselves out. I was so excited to be done setting up my office that when I closed the door behind me and reached for my car keys, I got that classic stomach-churning feeling you have when you realise…

"Oh fuck, I think my keys are still inside!"

Great way to finish my first day in business. I will forever be grateful for my friend. He saved me by letting me stay the night at his place and driving me in early the next morning to talk to the building manager. In sales you learn that everything that happens to you is 100% in your control, especially how you react to challenges and stressors. This was day one of my mental resilience training.

I could have freaked out and lost it, but I choose to stay positive. I had grown up a lot from that mediocre sales rep with an above-average dream that I had once been. I knew that if I stuck something out, it was always going to turn out okay. I mean, if locking myself out of the office on my first day as a branch manager was the worst thing that could happen, the only way was up.

As the days turned into weeks and the weeks into months, I started to find my groove and my capacity for work grew. I would run two interviews a day, five days a week, and train staff from Thursday to Saturday. I would then come into the office on Sunday to help my receptionist make phone calls to book up my next week. I could have hired an extra person to help make the calls, but I believe that you should never hire out a job that you wouldn't do yourself.

My mantra over this period was, "I moved away for work, so I'd better work." I chose this sacrifice, I had better live up to it.

There were only two things I wanted for my office culture: fun and money. I knew that to develop office culture you need to *be* the culture, so I tried to emphasize both those things. For example, during one of our conferences I bought these green shirts with Porky Pig on them. He was wearing a monocle and a pimp-purple suit, and he held a top hat with bills in it. I made sure my team wore this shirt during the conference because I thought it was funny and authentic. It represented fun and money.

To develop an office culture I set up contests and goals. The rewards were monetary bonuses, food, or experiences. I even used contests as an incentive for my receptionist to see if she could book more appointments than me, and the more times I challenged her, the better she got at her job.

My confidence started to grow. Even though I'd been a subpar sales rep back home, the people I was hiring had no sales experience and looked up to me for guidance. I was their go-to guy if they had successes or failures. I was their coach, their senpai, and their mentor. It was surreal to teach a brand new rep and see them do better than I had when I first started. That promotion that took me 21 months to get was achieved by two of them before the summer ended.

I felt like I was finding success in the company as a manager. I started to hit company-wide contests where the prizes were scholarships, white-water rafting trips, limo rides, trips across the country, and even a trip to Ireland. I wanted it all. For the first time in my life I knew that when I really wanted something I was willing to work for it. It didn't matter what the challenges were going to be. If I set my mind to achieve it, I believed it was already mine.

The choices that I'd made were bearing fruit, and that risk I took at the start of the summer to take on the position had turned into real fun. It wasn't that I was doing a cost-benefit analysis, a SWOT analysis, or calculating the risks; I was having fun running a business in real-time.

Here's what I want you to do: calculate how much fun you could have each time you have to make a decision. A simple question I ask myself when I have a decision to make is, "How much fun will I have?" If I'm not going to have fun, I don't want to do it.

This is the most important step in calculating your risk-to-fun ratio. You'll probably attempt things even when they don't sound like fun. You'll do something over and over again until you truly acknowledge you don't enjoy it, even if you buy all the gizmos, gadgets, top-of-the-line programs, and equipment. None of that really matters anyway. If you enjoy something, and it's fun, everything else is secondary.

When I started to learn how to play guitar I was awful and it wasn't fun. However, as I felt myself getting better at scales, techniques, and theory, I unlocked the gates to guitar-playing fun forever. Now it will always be fun for me.

I have friends who have amazing equipment that I would love to own, but they never use it. What's the point of buying shit you aren't going to use? Who are you trying to flex on when you don't enjoy the money you're spending? Quit trying to impress people and instead infect them with your passion so they become a fan.

Find a hobby you can start and then get better at it. Just because you're a working professional doesn't mean you can't take on something silly or learn a skill that offers no big gains. Do something for fun. Trust me, when you hit a new level of skill, it gets even more fun. Find something that has progression and have fun with it. How long do you want to have fun? When do you want to achieve your fun? Write that down and work towards *your* idea of fun. Nobody owns your joy other than you. If you're not having fun, don't lock yourself out and them complain about it. Take the hit on the chin and keep trying.

Okay, so I shared with you the idea of fun without a monetary return. Now let's talk about fun that has a positive impact on your wallet.

The Grande Prairie office I was running was one of 30 offices the company had opened across Canada that summer. The company was flourishing and I started to climb up the sales ladder. I guess it points to my former mediocrity that nobody in the company, including myself, expected me to be very successful. Yet, as the top reps everyone expected to "win" started to falter, underdogs like me started to take over.

It turns out people who find success too soon can quickly get crushed by the weight of other people's judgments and opinions. If everyone thinks you're the Golden Child in whatever they think you're great at, the pressure to keep that reputation becomes intense. And when you can't, the bigger you are, the harder you fall.

By the end of the company's three-month hiring spree, I had hired 26 people. It was one of the smallest teams in Canada. For being a small dog though, we had a big bite. My team and I sold and sold. I taught my team what it's like to have fun and get paid for it. I insisted that if ever a customer offered any of them water, juice, or liquor, they should say, "Yes," because when a customer offers you something, it's a gesture that shows you are more than just a salesman to them. You need to make the most of that in sales, because nobody gives you anything if you're a stranger.

I taught my reps that unless you really don't want something, take it, always. I've been offered books, gift cards, gas cards, room-and-board, and vegetables from someone's farm. That's because these customers connected with me. If I'd been a total stranger that added no value to their lives, they wouldn't have let me past their door. As cheesy as it sounds, I literally walked into every appointment trying to make a friend, and that was the best part of my job. It truly made my life easier. I still have customers from 2010 that I talk to regularly.

By the end of the summer, my team of 26 sales reps was number one for productivity in the nation. In other words, everyone who worked under me made more money than any other sales rep in the company across all of Canada.

In August I was in my prime. My team was selling, I was selling and my office was climbing the rankings. I didn't want to stop working because I was truly enjoying myself. Every time I sat down with a new customer I already knew that they would never forget me. It didn't matter whether they purchased something or not – I was the Chinese kid who sold knives.

That month's paycheque was the highest I'd ever seen. I made over $10,000 that month selling knives. I was also the number one manager in Canada in personal sales. I won a trip to Montreal and a trip to Dublin, Ireland. My life changed at that point. It didn't matter what other people's success were. What mattered was that I was having fun and making money while making an impact by teaching others how to do the same. My ability to sell surprised so many people that I would get calls asking me what I had sold that day. Another branch manager called me one Friday night asking that question and I told him it was just over $8,000. "Holy shit!" was his response.

When you put the work into your "practical superpower" you become a hero to others through your skill. If you're witty, charismatic, and likeable, maybe you can also monetize this superpower by starting a YouTube channel, a podcast, or by selling a product or service you believe in. Find out what your practical superpower is, write it down, and ask yourself, "How can I monetize my ability?"

Let's say you have an amazing talent with music and you don't know how to share it with the world. If playing music is your passion, make it your superpower. Do open mics, make video tutorials, do covers, do anything that pays. When you figure out what you're amazing at and make money from it, the fun comes naturally.

I took a risk that summer to find success. Not only did I achieve that success, I learned a lot about myself when faced with challenges. When the summer ended, managers like myself and top reps were flown to Montreal for the awards banquet, where we dressed to the nines to accept our rewards. After all that work and effort I was the number three branch manager in Canada. It didn't matter to me that I didn't come in first place because the girl who did was from the same province as me and was an underdog too. No one expected her to win. Yet she earned the coveted Silver Cup trophy. And although those who got first and second place were applauded, another name kept coming up to accept award after award.

That name was mine.

It ended up being the Wilson Wong show. I got to share the stage with the top career sales professionals. I was recognised for my office sales, my personal sales, my achievements, and I even earned a first generation iPad, which had just been released that year. I had so many trophies, awards, and prizes on my table that I needed a friend to help me carry them all back up to my hotel room.

That summer's experiences did something to me. After yearning for significance and dealing with failure, I finally found an abundance of money and success. This overwhelmed me emotionally and I even cried because I was so fucking happy.

An endless stream of opportunities is presented to us every day. When we lack the skills to recognise them, they pass before our eyes without us even knowing until we take a step back and reflect. By then, it's too late. I often wonder how many opportunities people turn down because they are put off by another person's opinion, whether it be from their mom, dad, significant other, or their friends. But when you start saying yes to things, who knows where it will take you.

Being able to monetize your fun takes a lot of guts though. You need to be able to laugh at the failures and acknowledge your progress. Having fun will grow your bank account when your skills become equal to the value you add to others. If you're having fun, creating content, adding value, and inspiring others to take action, they will look up to you and want to support you and be a part of your community. The speed at which you achieve this money may take longer than you'd like, but if you just plug away slowly every day, every week, every month, you might one day catch yourself saying, "Wow, I did this?"

Remember, be patient, take risks, and always have fun!

Chapter Four Summary

- Make sure you calculate the amount of fun you'll have.
- If you're going to quit, you might as well quit when you're at the top.
- Skill-based jobs pay more than hourly jobs.
- Make sure to buy cheese and chocolate milk when you move out. They're really delicious.
- It's a lot more fun to have money in the bank than no money in the bank.
- Crying happy tears is super manly.

Chapter Five:

The Richest Homeless Person

The successes I had in the summer of 2010 skyrocketed my name in the sales world. I was 21 years old and my office had sold product worth $140,000 in 4 months with just 26 sales reps. I personally earned over $25,000 just in that summer. I had gone from being a terrible sales rep to being an influential person in our company across the country.

The leadership team then decided they wanted me to run an office in a bigger city. And when you are getting recognition by important people, it's hard to say no.

I felt like this was only the beginning of my journey. What I learned from being a shitty sales rep and then being recognised for my contribution to the company was you have to hold yourself accountable and meet the expectations of people that care for you in the business.

When you're at the top, however, you fall the hardest. I witnessed it over and over again when success came immediately to the newbies. When I had been in sales for a year I would hear about those who surpassed my total sales over that period within 10 days of starting. They overcame the struggles I went through when getting a sale like they were nothing. I looked up to these newbies that had it easy. If they kept it up they would take over the world. Yet, before most of them even truly got started, they would quit.

Why, when success came so easily?

Reflecting on my experience, two things come to mind: consistency and mental fortitude.

What I love about sales is how primitive the food chain is. If you sell a lot, you are a top dog, but if you don't sell shit, you are just another member of the pack. It's how much you sell over 52 weeks, not just over 10 days, that really counts. Quick success allows a newbie to get instant gratification in the form of money, prizes, company recognition, and a rise in the office rankings. The reps that had immediate success took shortcuts to learning approaches and scripts, but this failed them in the long term. They just wanted to make money without ever really having a bigger goal in mind. Money alone will only motivate you for so long.

Even when I was going through the lacklustre start to my sales career, I wasn't doing it for the money. It was a lot of fun learning from some of the best sales reps in the company and hearing their stories. All I wanted was to get better, and eventually the skills I developed through that attitude rewarded me.

My advice: be consistent with your short-term goals and be open to whatever creative ways you think of that can help you obtain them. Each little milestone will grow your confidence in whatever you're doing. This is what motivated me through the bad days and allowed me to celebrate the successes I later earned.

The company always wanted to promote new managers. They would hype up the next big company trip to give the new managers a goal to work towards. The reward for sales managers who did the most business in the summer of 2011 was a trip to Maui, Hawaii. Having earned a trip to Ireland the year prior, I expected to go on this one, and I was excited to share it with my girlfriend.

They announced the trip in January and I was going to manage a new office starting in April. I went through the company's leadership and sales training program for a second time while still going to university. I sacrificed my evenings and weekends to train and practice my sales scripts.

Sales had taught me the art of negotiation. I remember telling my professors that I needed to fly to New York for a training seminar and asking if I could defer midterms to another day. They agreed, and when I arrived at my hotel I did some homework before going to talk to the new managers. I was extremely efficient and felt that running a business had taught me great time management skills for someone of such a young age.

April finally came and my girlfriend and I finished our final exams. We spent as much time together as we could before I left again for my "summer job." But this time my office wasn't just five hours away in Grande Prairie; it was a 16-hour drive across *two provinces* in Winnipeg, Manitoba.

Just before I left, I promised my girlfriend that I would take her to Maui no matter what. I was confident in my skills and ability to run another office, I meant every word of it. I packed my bags, stuffed my Toyota Camry with as much office furniture as I could fit in it and was off. My dad came with me this time so we could take turns driving. When we finally arrived in Winnipeg we spent a night at a motel. The next day I dropped my dad off at the airport and he flew back home, leaving me behind in a new city.

Luckily, I was close friends with the district manager for Winnipeg. She helped me with the transition, and between us we moved all the office supplies up two flights of stairs and set up the TVs and chairs. Then I was all set for another four-month grind.

Those four months passed in a flash, but not because the summer was just like the last one. Far from it.

My office failed.

I didn't hit the Top 10 and I lost close to $20,000. I went from a small town of 55,000 people and low expenses to a city with over

663,000 people and crushing overheads. I lived as frugally as I could, yet the cost of gas, rent, food, and the office lease had increased fourfold.

I was 21 years old, living two provinces away from my home, my office was bleeding money, I had no friends in the same city as me, and my business was failing. I was second guessing my judgement and wondering if I could keep my promise to take my girlfriend to Maui.

But I couldn't be negative. It was exhausting to bitch and complain. In our training we were taught to vent up, not down. That meant I would talk to my friends across the country who worked for the company and we would figure out a way for me to be as positive as possible.

My success the year before had taught me that when you work on your skillset, you will be profitable. But my failure this year wasn't one of skill. It was another lesson that I needed to learn: "Who is Wilson when shit hits the fan?"

So what did I do to get out of this rut?

I loved on others as hard as I could. I looked at the company standings and called my friends who were also on the cusp of failing. I was committed to bringing all of them up. Even though I was wounded, that didn't mean I couldn't carry others. I set up a system where we would watch movies in the theatre simultaneously across the country by coordinating time zones with showings in their cities. After each movie finished we would have a four-way call and nerd out on how awesome or awful it was. That helped build camaraderie and gave us all something to look forward to once a week. Together we watched a ton of movies and exchanged ideas about how to improve the business.

As that made me happier, my office started to grow. Why? It's simple: when you're happy at work, you get shit done. You also attract people who want to use and absorb your positive "aura." I was always ready to share mine.

When you lift others up, you lift yourself up. It can be lonely when you have to make an effort for other people and you can find yourself asking, "Why can't THEY put in the effort on me?" That's a selfish way of thinking. The best way to leverage your love to other people is to give it unconditionally. That doesn't mean you're a pushover. It means that when you decide to stop giving them that effort, you aren't losing them, they are losing you.

Making sales that summer was a battle, but I had a ton of fun fighting. I joined the university gym, asked my staff for fun places to go, and took the whole team out for team nights. I set up sales contests to motivate my team and paid for the prizes out of my own pocket. I started to build a cool culture that revolved around skills training. I decided that as a manager, I didn't have to miss out on the fun.

In the end, despite the struggles, it was an amazing summer! I stopped worrying about the money and started loving myself, my team, my colleagues across the city, and, most of all, the process of pulling it all together.

My office scraped into the company's top seven. I finished in the negative financially, but my mental currency was trading at an all-time high. Then, before I left for home, the company announced a contest in which the prize – a place on that trip to Maui – would go to anyone who sold $10,000 by the end of the summer.

With only 10 days left before summer ended, I knew this was my chance to keep that promise to my girlfriend. My office might have failed, but I knew how to do personal sales. I had no idea how I was going to hit the goal in 10 days, but I needed to do it. After the most gruelling four months of my life, the summer wasn't over.

I travelled back home and took a day to unpack and unwind. When my girlfriend came to visit I told her that my Winnipeg office didn't qualify for Maui and she took it well. Then I hit her with the news that we could still go if I just spent 10 more days doing what I did best: selling.

"Hey asshole, I haven't seen you in four months and you want to ditch me *again*," is what she could have said. But she knew I had good intentions. A promise is a promise and I knew that Maui would be the trip of a lifetime. 'They've given me a small window of opportunity and I'll fucking take it,' I was thinking.

The next day I went back to Grande Prairie to hit it big again. I had no idea where I was going to stay so I prepared for the worst – I packed four pillows, two blankets, a ton of utensils, a giant ass bowl, and a flat of bottled water so I could live out of my car.

Why did I do this to myself? Because I had made a promise to someone I cared about and I would do whatever I had to do to keep it. Part of me also thought it would be funny, ridiculous, and downright silly to live in a car for a week just so I could go on a trip. Mostly though, it was my way of showing myself that I had the audacity to risk being a fool and suffer discomfort to have a taste of success again.

It was also an opportunity to get creative. I didn't want to pay for a hotel because I could not afford one and I didn't know anyone in town, but all I needed were the necessities. My car was my shelter, but I also needed food, somewhere to shower and get ready to meet clients, and internet access to enter my sales orders.

The first thing I did was go to the college gym and purchase a prorated membership. It was only $20 for the month of August and that gave me the use of the showers and washrooms every day from morning until late in the evening. It gave me a chance to work out too and be that guy you couldn't kick out at closing time because I was taking a shower naked.

My number two strategy was leeching all my internet from Starbucks. Every morning I made my sales call from a Starbucks and logged into their free Wi-Fi. The staff soon got to know me and they didn't mind if I hung out for an hour or two in the morning and returned periodically throughout the day. Then, late at night, I would drive to the Starbucks parking lot, connect to their internet, and enter all my sales data from that day. God bless you, Starbucks. I couldn't have done it without you.

My third strategy was to bring this giant bowl. Since I couldn't keep anything cold I had only non-perishables, like a jumbo pack of cereal and canned soups But every morning I would go to the supermarket and buy one of those 250 ml cartons of milk and eat cereal with milk in my car out of that giant bowl. For protein I bought meat from the deli every day, and when I needed to heat up my soup, I would take my bowl to the food court to use staff microwave.

The last big challenge was deciding where to sleep. I couldn't sleep in the mall parking lot because security would get suspicious when they saw a single car parked there. I didn't want to sleep too far outside of the city either, because the college gym was downtown and close to the grocery store. So I did what I thought was logical and parked in a residential area near a playground.

Since it was an older neighbourhood I thought there wouldn't be a lot of children playing at the playground, so I parked in a neutral position where it looked like I could be a guest at one of the houses. It wasn't glamorous, but it did the trick and it helped me to keep telling myself, "It's only for a few more days. I can do this."

That positive self-talk carried me through the shitty sales days and reminded me that the pain was temporary and the reward would be worth it. Each morning I woke up at around 6:30 am, drove around downtown for a bit and then went to my headquarters at Starbucks. I'd get a coffee, turn on my laptop, organize my leads sheet, and then make calls. I booked as many appointments for the next few days as I could, starting as early as possible to maximize the amount of appointments I could do in a day.

I would do my first two appointments in the morning, then go to the grocery store and eat a pre-packaged kale salad, cereal, and cooked meat. I would then do my afternoon appointments, go back to the grocery store, buy supper, eat it, and drive back to Starbucks to make more phone calls and enter whatever sales I had made so far that day. After I finished the paperwork, I went to my evening appointments, which were usually at around 9:00 pm. Finally, my day ended with a trip to the gym, working out on the bike or doing a run on the treadmill before lifting some weights to give me the energy to do the things I would need to do the next day.

After only four days I was halfway towards my goal. I knew I couldn't let up. All I had to do was be homeless for just a little longer. And to reward myself I purchased a movie ticket to a late show. That got me bonus shelter until 1:30 am and it was exactly what I needed.

I followed the same routine every day until the seventh day.

On that day I surpassed my goal. In seven days I made over $6,000 in commissions, which I figured meant I was probably the richest homeless person in the city. And nobody knew except me. It also meant I could go home and tell my girlfriend that we would be going to Maui. The few people in the company who knew what I had been doing were in awe. Everyone else thought it was a "Wilson" thing.

"He's just good at selling," they said.

The truth is, for those seven days, I left myself with no choice but to be good at selling. Being homeless made me aware of what I'm good at and what I'm not. For the first time in my life, I was truly proud of myself. Nobody could ever take this experience away from me. It was mine to keep.

It's safe to say that my bank account didn't grow that summer, but I grew in resiliency. Learning about what I could achieve, even in the face of adversity, was a gift to myself that I cherish. Also, Maui turned out to be one of the greatest trips of my life so far. I do not regret anything.

Chapter Five Summary

- Sometimes you need to be at the bottom to appreciate what you earn when you're at the top.

- Remember to set a goal before you're homeless or else you're just homeless without a goal and that's silly.

- When you are homeless, remember to buy a gym membership, find a good park to sleep at, and leech Wi-Fi off Starbucks.

- Once you're done being homeless, go to Maui and ball out.

- Don't give up.

Chapter Six:

The Anti-Fun Police: My Three-Year Prison Sentence

I believe that right now people in their 20's are facing a struggle. If you follow our society's "ideal", it looks something like this:

1. After high school you go into university or college.
2. By 22 you should have a degree.
3. After university you work and you love the work you're doing.
4. You work hard for seven years, make money, find a partner, buy a house, and get married.
5. At 30 you start a family.
6. You continue to work and love your job until the day you die.

At one point this all sounded pretty good to me. Then I realised it was not the path I was meant to take.

I was never an academic. I was always a B-grade student. I even failed a class in university and had to be put on probation. It took me five years to graduate. I had a major in Psychology and a minor in General Business. But basically I paid $30,000 for a piece of paper that said, "Good for you. You're competent enough to sit still for five years. Now pay back your loan."

When I graduated in 2013, I was 23 years old. I had an undergraduate degree and five years of sales experience under my belt. I learned far more in those five summers selling than I did in school. It was a paid internship on how to run a business and interact with people.

However, my professional life started to stagnate once I left school.

My district manager moved on from the company, we no longer had a leader. My friends in the business either graduated, moved to a new city, or quit the job. All my work friends were leaving. I thought it was normal, so I decided to follow the trend. I quit too.

I had some time to travel so I decided to visit San Francisco and Los Angeles with my girlfriend. eSports was a growing phenomenon and, as a big gamer in university, one of my favourite online games was *League of Legends*. I watched the Season 3 World Championships in California and my friend Lance tagged along. It was one of the best nerd trips I've ever done. Lance and I swore that wherever the Season 4 World Championships were held, we would be there. Not long after, it was announced that they would be in South Korea.

When I returned home from California, however, reality set in. I was going to have to get a "real" job.

An old sales colleague was working at a well-known investment firm and told me that I should apply. If I got the job he would get a $500 bonus, so it would be a win for both of us. Besides, I'd almost burned through my financial resources and the "Empty" light was about to come on. I went through the online application process, used my friend's name as a referral, and received a call for an interview very soon after.

I had been at the highest level of sales and development before I left my knife-selling job. I'd run two offices in western Canada as well as recruited and trained my own staff. Because I could talk about anything and everything involved in sales, I was sure when I went for this interview that I would get the job.

The investment team had two partners, which meant I had to be interviewed twice. The first interview went so well that I got hugged at the end of it. For the second interview they gave me a task, which was to research a topic and present it. That was literally my job as a sales rep – sit down with customers, present a product, handle objections, and then close. Easy. Because of that, I nailed the task.

It was a happy New Year for me at the start of 2013 when I began the onboarding process, keen to learn about money. It was lots of fun learning something new and at a high level. I was given the role of marketing guy with the team, which entailed working on presentations for my advisors, making follow up phone calls to clients, and pushing paper here and there. I got to stock the desk in my cubicle with all the free notebooks, planners, and pens I could fit in it. I even added some photos to personalize it. I was living the classic corporate life, attending business networking meetings, lunch-and-learns, and charity galas. For the first six months I loved it.

Then something changed.

My shift was from 10:00 am to 6:00 pm, Monday to Friday. The late start meant I could sleep in a little. Yet, because I was in a cubicle all day, it was dark when I left at night, especially in the winter. My cubicle was in the far back corner where my advisors couldn't really notice if I was there or not. So over time I started to come in 15 minutes late and leave 15 minutes early.

Why?

Because the job was not fulfilling. There were no goals for me to pursue. I would sit there and try to get motivated by making up the dumbest goals I could think of. On one occasion I set out to finish two PowerPoint presentations and reward myself with a cup of coffee. But I could get one of those for free at any time in the staff kitchen. Another time I showed my advisor why we needed better mice for the computers. She ended up buying two: one for her and one for me.

I realized that by going from a job with freedom to a job with stability, I was wasting time on dumb shit.

If you love your job, or at least you're growing, learning, and getting paid well, keep doing it. I didn't love my job, and I wasn't getting any of those things.

It definitely wasn't that I didn't want to work. When I was in sales, I chose to do 80-hour weeks when I was motivated. No one told me what I could and couldn't do, so if I wanted to do nothing, I did just that. I knew the consequences of slacking off were that my business would suffer and I would fail.

In the corporate world though, everything was routine. I worked 40 hours a week from 10:00 am to 6:00 pm, Monday to Friday. I would take a 15-minute break at noon, lunch at 2:00 pm, and another break near the end of the day. It was an awful pattern. I knew EXACTLY what I was going to do every single day. There was no variety and no opportunities for spontaneity. It was incredibly boring.

The worst part for me was that I knew exactly how much money I was going to make. It didn't matter how hard or how little I worked, the paycheque was always the same.

Something I took away from this experience was this:

If you slack, you fear being fired, which means you put pressure on yourself, stress even more, and become less confident in your abilities. How can you help your employer grow their business when you're just trying to survive?

Though if you work really hard, you might get a bonus at the end of the year. But is it really worth the late nights and overtime that you didn't want to claim because you felt bad that you didn't finish

100 hours' worth of work in 40? Oh wait, that should be 35 hours because you had to take your lunch break (although, if you're like my friends in the corporate workforce, you work through your lunch because you need to get X done, and you don't really have time to eat because you are, "Oh so busy").

With this mindset, I stopped caring about my job. Don't get me wrong, when there was work to be done I did it to the best of my ability. I take pride in my work even if it's mundane. But I wanted to have fun too.

However, just because I wasn't happy at my job didn't mean I burned any bridges. I take the phrase, "It's not what you know, it's who you know," very seriously. Therefore, to find fun, I did what I do best: I engaged with people.

I love connecting with people, and I genuinely care about what they have to say. I've found that if you ask specific, high quality, and engaging questions, people are more likely to help you out or just open up to you, even if they might not get anything out of it. Think of it this way, if you had a friend, cousin, niece, or nephew ask you a good question, would you answer them or just look at them in a funny way and walk away? When someone asks you a high quality or specific question, it makes you feel special because you are top of mind for them. When you're top of mind to somebody, you're probably more than willing to answer their questions. Plain and simple.

Some of my colleagues at the investment firm were brilliant, and I needed to take advantage of that. I spoke with everyone and anyone in my office whom I thought I could add value to. I particularly went for people who never got appreciation even though they deserved it. That was usually the receptionists, not the millionaire advisors. Why? Well, I literally saw them every day. They transferred calls, ordered office supplies, kept the kitchen in order, and did many other small tasks that, in my opinion, were some of the most important things done in the office (especially organizing the staff lunches, because I *love* eating).

Becoming friends with the front-end staff meant my days started brightly. I was always greeted with a smile and a conversation as I headed into the office. If I wanted to order a specific office supply, I got friendship priority and it was ordered right away. When it came to food for the office, my favourite foods would magically appear in the kitchen.

Being able to talk to anyone and pick brains was the best thing I could have done for myself in those circumstances. Since I was in the banking world, I wanted to learn how to make money work for myself. As I went around asking questions, the advisors and assistants talked to me about topics like property investments, stocks, and the market. The assistants, meanwhile, taught me how to use different programs and resolve common issues.

I was starting to have fun at my job, and wasn't ready to give up just yet. There was still lots to learn from the people around me, plus they never really gave me an excuse to quit.

That is, until they decided to not let me go to Korea.

When I was hired, I mentioned that I was planning to go to Asia in October and we verbally agreed that I would be able to go. I had my flights, hotel, and tickets purchased because it was an experience I wasn't going to miss. Naively, I believed that they had given me their irrevocable permission.

I was wrong about that.

"Wilson, we need you to stay here at the office on these dates," my boss told me two weeks before my trip. "We have a big client event happening and we need you."

"I'm taking my vacation in Asia on those dates, I won't be here," I protested. "Are you telling not to go on this trip?"

"Wilson, I can't have you leave during the client event," my boss insisted. "But you can go after."

I cannot describe how upset I was. My face was stoic and my body language was neutral, but I was fuming. Then I went back to my desk, committed to this ultimatum: work or leave.

I googled, "How to write a letter of resignation." I copied the template, wrote all the necessary details, and stuffed my letter in an envelope. But I did not hand it in immediately. I knew I needed time to reflect. I went home, still mad and restless, told my girlfriend what happened and talked with my mom. They asked the same thing.

"What will you do?"

"Quit," I said. "Final answer."

"What are you going to do after you're back from the trip?" they both asked me.

"I'll figure it out," I said.

Neither my mom nor my girlfriend tried to convince me to stay in the job. They knew that if I was unhappy, I could make a decision for myself. Besides, I told them I would figure it out, and I always did.

Deciding to quit caused something crazy to happen. I was happy. I felt relief, calm, and a sense of confidence. I felt like I had regained control over my life. I wasn't somebody else's peon or workhorse. I was in total control of my life again.

It wasn't over just yet though. I still needed to hand in my resignation letter to HR the next day.

On the day I quit I went in early, walked downstairs to the Human Resources office, put my letter in the mailbox, and went back to my desk to clean it out. Halfway through doing that my telephone rang. It was the head of HR and she asked me to come down to her office.

When I got there she asked me a ton of questions, but in the end she couldn't convince me to reconsider. I went back to my desk and finished packing everything into a box. It was like a scene out of a movie. At some point I got a call from my advisor. She didn't want to see me, and I didn't want to waste her time. We had a quick exchange of words and I hung up. Then I said my goodbyes around the office and left. I was free.

Although that job wasn't for me, I'm very grateful for that experience. It helped me figure out what I like about a job and what I don't. I also enjoyed learning about investing and how to grow money. Most importantly though, I learned that by finding ways to take advantage of my circumstances and environment, I can make it fun.

Going to Korea was also one of the most influential experiences of my life. The World Championship was only one day, but in the two weeks that I was there I created some of my best memories. It was the beginning of a journey to figuring out who I was and what I wanted to become, something I would never have got sitting in a grey cubicle stuck to a set schedule.

Quitting my job and traveling was truly great, but when I came back from my vacation reality set in again. I needed to find another J.O.B.

I had money in the bank so I decided I could afford to take my sweet time finding work. In the meantime, I tried to have as much fun as possible. I hung out with my girlfriend, played video games with my internet friends, worked on my health, began powerlifting, and dabbled in parkour. I also touched on my creative side. I started making music, practising drumming, and refining my guitar techniques. I tried numerous things that did not bring home the bacon, but I loved it all.

A few months later my friend Will asked me if I wanted to go to the Consumer Electronics Show in Las Vegas. Will is one of the most interesting people I know. He is extremely intelligent and business savvy. In school he started a ramen shop and later he worked at an insurance company while running a battery business on the side. Did I mention that he can also speak four languages and is the Vice President of the Fukienese Association in Edmonton? Yet he's still extremely humble and quiet.

CES is a four-day trade show where you can see the newest technology before it hits store shelves. When Will asked me if I wanted to check it out, I knew he was planning on doing big things. As the preceding chapters might have hinted, when I see an opportunity, I'll take it. I got my tickets, booked my flight and we were off.

As it turned out, that trip to Vegas was awful. I got sick and developed a ton of blisters on my hands and feet. The smell of strong perfume and cigarettes gave me headaches and nausea. To top it off, one of the quietest people I know snored in his sleep. At first I made fun of the fact that his snoring was louder than his voice. But it stopped being funny when I realized that he was getting perfect sleeps every night while I was getting yelled at by his nose.

Even though the trip bombed, on a personal level it was one of the most significant trips I've done. Having five days with my friends gave me a lot of time to share stories. Near the end of the trip I mentioned to Will that I needed to find a job and he said he would check around for me when we got back.

Two weeks after we returned, Will texted me to check my email. I'd received a referral link to the insurance company he worked for. The application process was the same as the bank. I attached my resume and cover letter, answered the questionnaire, and sent everything off.

A few days later I got called in for an interview. This time I didn't get a hug at the end of the interview, but I was hired on the spot.

I can't say I was very excited about this new chapter in my employment history, but I thought it would be fun to learn about insurance, and it would allow me to be useful. I knew I would gain some good knowledge and skills, plus I could work with a good friend. Also, having had two car accidents in my life, I thought it would be great to know how to deal with them if I were to ever have another.

Speaking of those two accidents, the first was because my dumb ass didn't clean all the frost and snow off my windshield. I was going to be late for class, so I tried doing the duck-and-drive while the windows defrosted (everyone does this in cold weather). I ended up hugging the right side of the residential road too much and crashed into a snowbank. I'm lucky that I didn't hit a person or another car, but the right passenger side bumper was smashed and I broke the windshield wiper fluid container. I remember looking at it and thought, 'I'm an idiot, I was going to be late for class anyway.' My parents weren't happy with the incident

but we ended up getting cheap aftermarket parts to fix it.

My second accident was when I was working at the bank during a statutory holiday. I wanted some extra time-and-a-half pay. I parked in the parkade and went up to work. Once the workday was over and I started to approach my car, a security guard approached me and told me there was an accident that involved my vehicle. From where I was standing there was no damage. That was until I walked to my driver side door and it was completely crunched in. I gathered all the information and went on with my day.

As with any new job, the honeymoon phase at the insurance company was the best. I got six weeks of paid training and I learned a ton about vehicle, home, and commercial insurance. When training was over, I was a full-fledged insurance auto adjuster. This meant when someone was in an accident, they would call me. I would then set up a tow truck and a rental and tell the caller whether they were at fault for the accident.

It was a lot more fun than corporate banking. The company treated everyone extremely well. We had free lunches a few times a month and they had ping-pong tables in the lunchrooms. And the best part was that I was surrounded by good people.

Or so it seemed.

It wasn't long before I started to hate my job again. This time it wasn't boredom but the work environment. Everyone was miserable. They would bitch and complain about everything. I hated that. They were so negative that I started to believe that this was going to be my life.

"Woe is me, my life is hard, and everyone is out to get me!"

Though I couldn't really blame them. The workload was heavy and the amount of claims we had to take in a day was ridiculous. This was the first job that caused me stress from having to do too much work. On top of simple motor vehicle accidents, we had to deal with complicated claims about arson or stolen vehicles. I was handling over 300 claims at a time and every one of the claimants wanted me to deal with their shit first.

What followed were not some of my proudest moments in this life. I went from being the most positive and uplifting person to having anger issues. I struggled every day to be happy and not break something. But at various times I smashed my keyboard, broke my desk, and punched my computer monitor clean in the face. I had to talk with my manager about that one.

I had hissy-fits in the men's washroom fighting the paper towel dispenser, and one time I smashed the elevator button and it made a loud banging sound that made my claims manager come out of her office to check what happened. I said nothing.

I was not in a good headspace at work and when I got home I wouldn't say "Hi" to anyone in the house. I went straight to my room to play video games. I needed escapism to deal with the next day. I barely talked to my girlfriend because there was nothing to say other than how shitty my day was.

Then a friend of mine, JT, who had never given up our sales gig, came to visit me in my hometown. He had gone from being a branch manager to district manager of one of the largest cities in our company and earning over six figures. I went out for lunch with him and another mutual friend and we spent hours talking and catching up. When he asked me how my job was going I told him the truth. It sucked!

He asked me how much I was making and, having no shame, I told him. Being one of the nicest assholes I know, JT told me what I needed to hear. He told me that he paid more in taxes than I made in a year. That fucking hurt.

When your close friend shits on you like that you can either attempt to salvage what's left of your pride and ego by calling them a dick and disowning them as a friend, or you can accept what they say as the truth. I did the latter. Then JT said something else that changed everything.

"Come on, Wilson, you're better than that. Come back to sales. Quit your job and move down to my city to sell with my office."

Those words would change my attitude towards my insurance job completely. But I couldn't say yes to JT at the time. I stuck with the insurance job through the Christmas holidays and at the corporate Christmas party I drank and enjoyed myself.

At that point JT had been talking about his company trip to St. Kitts in the Caribbean. I had no idea where that was, but he asked me if I wanted to go. Since I'd been on sales company trips with him I knew how much fun they were. Nevertheless, I politely declined. JT kept pushing it though. He told me that he made a bet with his division manager that he could get me back selling. That's when he dropped the bomb: he would pay for me to go.

"Come hang out," he said. "Relax and talk with our national and divisional sales managers."

I couldn't refuse. If this was him bribing me to come back, so be it. I said yes and made my vacation arrangements.

That trip was everything I expected. I hung out in the sun and spent time with the top-selling managers from all over Canada. I was surrounded by positivity and encouragement. It was amazing.

Like JT, the national and divisional managers believed that I would make an impact. They knew my history and told me that if I came back, there would be a lot of support for me.

I'd always wanted to have amazing people truly believe in me. Having the ability to trust someone's judgement of me even when I didn't believe in myself made me a better person. There was a difference between Mom and Dad telling me they believe in me and a friend putting his money where his mouth is and taking me across the world to show me that he does.

I needed to quit my job and work for myself, but not by myself. I needed to go back to the sales company where I had excelled, where I would be among people who would celebrate my highs and support me through my lows. That was the environment I thrived in.

I went back to work feeling refreshed and reinvigorated. Two weeks later, however, I was back in low mode with the threat of being fired because of my lack of speed and my anger.

I had my performance review that week where I met with my unit manager. We began our meeting with small talk about how my trip was. Then she took out my insurance stats and started talking about where we can improve and yadda, yadda, yadda. I understood everything but it went in one ear and out the other.

Then something inside me snapped.

I remember turning to my unit manager and stopping her mid-sentence.

"I think I'm done."

"Sorry?" she answered, looking at me in shock.

"I'm done," I repeated.

"What do you mean you're done?" she responded.

"I don't want to work here anymore," I said flat out. "Consider this my two weeks' notice." Then I smiled.

I had done it again. I quit my job. Only this time I did it mid-sentence and without a letter.

My parents were used to me quitting so my talk with them was easy. I told them I was going to move away and go back into sales. They didn't bat an eye. They knew I was trying to find myself as a person and they let me do whatever I wanted.

Telling my girlfriend that I had to move away was more difficult. I told her how unhappy I was with the insurance job and that I needed to quit. She didn't want me to go again and she started to cry. I explained to her that the longer I stayed in an unhappy place, the worse I would become. I needed to leave for my own sake.

I promised that I would come visit when I got a chance and call her every day. I don't know how many times I said sorry, but I needed to be selfish and take a chance on myself. I had been so unhappy for the past two years that I needed to do it.

Two weeks later I moved three hours south from Edmonton to Calgary. I roomed with JT and started selling again. I got off to a slow start but it was like riding a bicycle. By the end of the year I was the number three sales rep in Canada. I figured that was not bad after a three-year hiatus.

I had finally broken out of my prison. I had given the corporate world three years of my life and I didn't want to give it any more. I promised myself that I would never go back. It stifled my creativity, ruined my ability to set goals and dream big, and made me become self-loathing, angry, and negative. Never again.

My saving grace was the belief that others had in me. So, please, if you truly believe in someone, show them, because you might change their life for the better.

Chapter Six Summary

- The honeymoon phase is just that, a honey phase. Once it's over, you need to figure what you're really about.

- Treat the job you hate as a "paid internship" to learn more about yourself.

- Fighting the paper dispenser or the elevator doesn't get you a raise at work.

- Give yourself a chance to see if you like the job or not. You can always just quit on the spot.

- Prioritize your own happiness or else you'll just drag everyone around you down. Don't be that guy or gal.

Chapter Seven:

Optimism is About Getting Lost

Since travelling is a norm in my family I have never worried about getting lost. To me it would be like finding a $20 bill in your jacket pocket that you never wear – unexpected, but pretty awesome. I have friends who map out everything when they travel, day by day, hour by hour, but I'm the type of guy who just shows up and plays it by ear.

For example, one day when I was in Korea to watch the *League of Legends* World Championships I got a chance to explore the market across from our Airbnb. Before I left I arranged with my girlfriend and other friends to meet up again in the early evening.

I decided it would be pretty cool to get a haircut while I was there and surprise everyone when I turned up looking handsome and all. It was late in the afternoon but the sun was still shining and I figured I had loads of time. I stopped to watch some of the student buskers and got a snack at a food cart.

As I was searching for a barber the sun started to set. 'No problem,' I thought, 'I'll quickly get a haircut and be on my way. I'm an experienced travelling salesman, I don't need a GPS; I'll use landmarks. The fried chicken shop is over there and the main street is that way.'

When I eventually found a barber it was a tiny hole-in-the-wall shop. It even had that red, white, and blue spinning thing outside that barbers have in Canada. When I walked into the shop, I was greeted by an old Korean man. It didn't matter that I couldn't speak the language, I pretended to cut my own hair and he got the message. He handed me a trendy Korean magazine and I flipped through it until I found a simple haircut. The dude took his sweet time getting started but once he did I really enjoyed it.

It turns out that when they wash your hair in Korea you're facing downwards and not the ceiling like you do in Canada. Basically the barber shoved my face into a big ass sink. Whatever. I just relaxed, enjoyed the silence, and lost track of time.

The trouble was, by the time he finished and I had paid, the market and the street had completely changed. I walked out and felt like I was in a completely different city. The streets were alive and music was playing at various stores. New carts were popping up and it was starting to get busy.

I scratched my head and said to myself, "Oh shit, this isn't good."

I thought I had walked up the street and turned left into the barbershop, so I figured I just needed to do the reverse to get back to where I was staying.

It was an enjoyable walk, and since I was confident in where I was going I figured I would explore a little. And then bam! One moment I was in a busy area, and the next, after making a few turns, there was literally nobody around me. It was like something out of a movie. There was no noise, just silence.

At this point I had another "Oh shit" moment. I walked back to where I thought I had come from, through another alley, and again there was dead silence around me.

"Uh-oh," would have been an understatement.

I stood there just pondering what I should do. I needed to find someone to help me but I couldn't speak Korean. What I did have was an app on my phone. All I needed was access to free Wi-Fi but, you guessed it, there was nothing. Who thought it would be okay to not purchase an internet plan while overseas?

Rather than just stand there like an idiot, I started walking down the street looking through the app to see if there was a word for train station. Our Airbnb was in front of one so all I needed was to find where the nearest one was.

Being lost is like being put in a pressure cooker. Everything you do and see feels heightened. I wasn't going to die, but I also didn't want to be "that guy" who got lost and had to be brought back to his Airbnb by the police.

By getting lost I had to really immerse myself in the environment. I started looking at things in great detail. I started recognizing streets I had walked through six times. I loved it.

When I approached strangers on the street, I told them in English that I was lost, said "train station" in Korean and pointed around. They sent me in a certain direction and the more I asked for directions, the more I got to explore. I found lots of restaurants and cool little shops selling trinkets that I would never have seen if I'd gone to a restaurant I'd googled. Eventually I recognized where I was and got back to the Airbnb. Turns out I went in the opposite direction of where I needed to go from the barbershop.

My friends had no idea what I'd just gone through. To them everything was normal but I had just gone through fear, nervousness, and anxiety. If I'd doubted myself and become negative, there would be no way I would have enjoyed that walk as much as I did. Yet I came back in one piece and just in time to leave with my friends for dinner.

This is why I compare getting lost to finding $20 in your pocket. That experience was one of the biggest highlights of my trip to Korea and it was completely unexpected. Because it is in those moments of clarity when you realize you're lost that cause you to either fold under the pressure, or dig deep and figure something out (I give myself bonus points for being able to take my friends to a trendy Korean restaurant that I found while I was lost).

I don't only get lost in foreign countries though.

When I was still in university, my girlfriend's sister and brother-in-law would go to this small town beach about an hour away from where I lived. She said she'd like to go there with me so we packed a cooler full of drinks and some food and left early on a Saturday morning.

When we were near the beach I realised that nothing was open until 9:00 am. The town was so small that if you drove down the main street very far you'd pass the town entirely. As we were heading to the beach I missed the exit and needed to do a U-turn. Since the single road highway wasn't wide enough for me to do one in my sedan, I drove down a farm road that was also too narrow. I ended up driving all the way to the farm, and as I was pulling up I saw two women sitting on the porch. Then a dog came running up to the car, which caused me to stop.

That could have been an awkward situation with the two women having watched me deliberately drive all the way up to the farmhouse for no apparent reason. To try to prevent that, however, I did what I know best: I rolled down the window.

"Good morning," I said. "How are you today."

My girlfriend didn't say anything. She just watched me from the passenger seat.

"Good morning," one of them said. "We're well. Can we help you with something?"

"Yes, we were planning to visit the town but there nothing is open," I explained. "I was trying to U-turn but here I am."

Both ladies chuckled and asked what we were going to do that morning. I mentioned that we were going to the beach to hang out and explore the town. Then, since we had nothing else to do, I threw out a question.

"My girlfriend and I have never been on a farm. Could we explore yours to kill some time?"

There was a pause and the ladies looked at each other.

"Sure, why not?" one said.

"Sweet! Thank you so much," I responded.

I had honestly never been on a farm. Even when I was selling knives it was usually at residential properties. I rarely went out selling in the boonies.

I rolled up my window, looked at my girlfriend, and chuckled.

As I got out of my car I was greeted by the large dog and I patted him on the head. We walked up to the ladies and introduced ourselves. They were mother and daughter and the daughter was visiting that morning. Just like I learned in sales, I made it my goal to ask questions about them and tell them a bit about ourselves. As with any presentation, it was a process of give and take.

I told them I was going to university and working part-time selling knives, which I was still doing at that time. We were invited to sit on the patio furniture and we chatted for a while. It was remarkable how cool the mom and daughter were with us being there. They asked what we wanted to do after school and what made us come all the way to the beach. What I thought was going to be a quick "Hello" and "Goodbye" ended up being a complete morning with the family.

As lunchtime approached, the mom asked us if we wanted to stay. We had nothing else to do, so we were more than happy to.

"Since you haven't been on a farm before let us show you how we do things here," the mother said. "Would you like to pick the vegetables from the garden?"

My girlfriend and I looked at each other and agreed that it would be great.

As the mom took us to the garden the daughter started up the barbeque. We walked down the deck and around the corner to one of the biggest gardens I'd ever seen. They had everything. You name it, they were growing it. The mom directed us to pick some vegetables and I took my camera out to document the moment. It ended up being a cool experience for both of us.

Once we were done picking enough vegetables for everyone, we went inside to wash them. Then, as we set the patio table for lunch, they asked me what kind of sales I was doing. I told them I sold knives. They asked if I had any pocket knives. The mom mentioned that her husband had been looking for a good pocket knife so maybe, when he came back, he could look at what I had.

'Is this really happening?' I thought. 'Am I about to make a sale because I missed my exit and ended up on someone's property because I couldn't do a U-turn on the road and then got invited to eat lunch with them?'

But it was literally unfolding before my eyes.

Once the food was ready we sat and talked into the early afternoon. Our conversation was interrupted when the husband drove up. He was surprised he had guests. The women told him what happened and he chuckled and introduced himself. Then he walked into the kitchen, grabbed himself a plate, and sat with us. He got a chance to get to know us and his wife mentioned that I was selling knives he might be interested in.

"Sure, let's see what you've got," he said.

I went to my car, pulled out my catalogue, and explained the features, benefits, and the guarantee to him. He flipped through it, and when he got to the pocket knife section he pointed at one of the black-handled knives and said, "I'd like one of these, please."

"Yes sir," I replied with no hesitation.

I wrote up an order then and there and we carried on talking. After lunch we said goodbye, hugged, and took a photo together. The picture turned out awful but it was one of my most memorable photos to date.

When we left the farm my girlfriend and I didn't say much at first. I just remember her laughing at how random the encounter was. We went into town, played mini-golf, and finally went to the beach where we ate ice cream. It ended up being an eventful vacation because I went the wrong way.

Being optimistic is the key when you get lost, whether literally or figuratively. It gives you feedback on how you feel about where you're at and applies just as much to your goals, dreams, and aspirations as it does to geography. Sometimes the things you plan for in life don't go according to plan. Maybe you didn't get into your desired college, or you didn't get that dream job. Nevertheless, you need to try to see the light in every situation. By relying on the light of optimism, you will find something inside you that will allow you to push forward even though you might not know what will happen next.

Sometimes the best things that happen to us are things we didn't account for. You never know when someone will walk into your life and make a massive impact on you, or when you'll be that person for someone else. Just remember, you have 100% control over your ability to see the best in yourself and any situation you find yourself in.

Chapter Seven Summary

- If you get lost, embrace it. But also make sure you buy a data plan.
- Getting lost at night is definitely worse than getting lost during the day.
- When you're stuck between a dog and an awkward place, just say hello and introduce yourself.
- Vegetables grown and handpicked from the garden are really tasty.
- Sometimes (but not always) you might be able to make some commission by attempting a U-turn.

Chapter Eight:

Backstage with Initiative

On top of selling knives, I'm currently working as Events Director for a non-profit organization called the Front Row Foundation. My job is to give Front Row Experiences to individuals who are braving critical, life-threatening illnesses. These experiences are usually concerts, shows, and sporting events. Ever since I got this job everything I've done has been a trial by fire. I never got the proper training, so I've been executing my role at a good level, but it could be better. What's great about the role though is that it allows me to job-shadow other professionals all over the United States.

It's my responsibility to make events happen. That means I am the salesperson, negotiator, booking agent, travel agent, researcher, photographer, videographer, video editor, babysitter, and, most importantly, the VISA carrier. I'm the one who spends the charity's money.

What I love about this foundation is that 100% of the proceeds support the dreams of recipients. I do it because granting wishes and seeing people happy is amazing.

I am selfish when I do this job though. Why? Because I can't wait for those days when someone wants to see their dream band or celebrity and it just so happens to be my favourite band or celebrity too. I get to organize their dream meet-up and piggyback off it. How cool is that?

One wish I granted was for a gentleman in my hometown who had testicular cancer. He wanted to watch the local hockey team literally from the front row. Another was for a young woman in Montreal. I took her to see her favourite singer live at Madison Square Garden in New York City. Seeing how happy these recipients were and how their families reacted to their experiences was incredible. This is the kind of awesome stuff I do.

This job is extremely rewarding, but getting it was a difficult transition for me. My girlfriend of ten years left me just one month before I got a chance to grant my first wish. I was heartbroken, but I had people relying on me so I had to keep things straight. The break-up was a big deal to me, but the people I was granting wishes for were braving illnesses and I wasn't going to give up on them. Knowing I was making someone's day when they were fighting for their life gave me the strength to push forward with my own mental well-being.

Losing my best friend, lover, and significant other of over a decade totally fucking sucked. Professionally, I was living my best life. I was selling a ton of product, granting wishes, and starting side hustles. Yet my personal life was shitty and I cried more that year than I've ever cried. But when I look back at some of the wishes I've granted, I feel like my heartbreak was peanuts compared to what the people I was granting those wishes for, and their families, were going through.

My job requires me to prepare a recipient event that is customized to a specific person. I need to know everything about that person, so our recipients have to go through a pre-screening process. We ask them every personal question we can think of, down to things that may not even matter to some people. Not only do we need to know their prognosis, we want to hear about everyone in their family, plus things like their favourite restaurant, colour, and flavour of candy or chips. This information allows us to grant them a wish that is highly personalized.

When I granted my first wish it was such an amazing experience to see how strong the family was and how their community rallied behind them. It made me realise how grateful I should be for being healthy. That day changed how I look at life, how I react to the environment and the people around me.

After the second wish I realised I should be grateful to be able-bodied. I was working with a young woman who could not walk but had the courage and the strength to pursue her dreams despite that. 'Who the fuck am I to complain if my body is feeling a bit tired or sore?' I thought. Her desire to not let her disability define her was incredible. Meeting her taught me how to respect my body. You'll never hear me complaining about aches and pains because those will pass. Being paralyzed from the chest down doesn't.

When Front Row's Chairman and I discussed when we could grant our third wish for the year, an opportunity came up in the US to help with an event and get training done. After we hashed out the details, it turned out that the destination was, once again, New York City. This time the recipient loved Christmas and his family treated November and December as a two-month celebration.

Once all the plane tickets and hotels were booked I got the itinerary for the New York experience. It was late in the evening and I was working on the final details of the trip while listening to one of my favourite dance musicians, San Holo, on YouTube. I'd been listening to his latest album, *Album1*, on repeat for months, and often hoped he might perform in my city, and, since I was tired, I decided to procrastinate and check out San Holo's website to see if he was on tour. Every other time I'd checked there was never anything in Canada. Nevertheless, I googled his website and clicked on tour dates. There still wasn't anything in Canada, but then I looked at his other dates. And then I cross-checked it with my travel itinerary.

I paused in disbelief.

San Holo was actually going to be playing live in New York City when I was going to be there. Holy shit! I looked at the ticket prices and was even more blown away. It was only $25 to get in. Then I saw that for just $100 you could get a meet-and-greet with San Holo. I couldn't believe it. I had waited for him to come to my hometown and now I was going to meet him *in a week*.

I quadruple checked the time and date of the event and googled the venue. It was literally an eight-minute walk from where I would be staying. How could it have worked out any better? I was ecstatic. I went straight to my wallet, took out my credit card, and bought meet-and-greet tickets then and there.

Being able to arrange meet-and-greets is invaluable when I'm granting wishes. I get to see how happy people are when they interact with their favourite stars. With San Holo, I needed to take a page from my own playbook and make sure I got to experience this from the front row. I wanted to grant my own wish.

In life we often do cost-benefit analyses when we want to do something. We hum and haw and then suddenly realize that it's too late. That's what the Front Row Foundation is all about – making sure it's not too late for people whose wishes we can grant. That's why I wasn't going to miss the opportunity to meet one of my favourite artists. When I plugged in my credit card number for those tickets, I prayed to the internet gods to take my money so I could grant my own wish.

Life can throw crazy curves at you when you least expect them. You need to have the ability to recognise those occasions, and the courage to take advantage of opportunities when they come at you. With this third wish I was granting I was going to make an impact on the lives of a family in difficult circumstances and, as a bonus, I was going to get the chance to grant myself a wish for a mere $100 in New York City. At the time I couldn't fathom how insane this situation was. Leading up to the trip I was so excited that I couldn't sleep.

Fast forward to the day of the concert.

I had made sure I booked flights that left extremely early even before I found out about the concert so I would have some time to kill before my recipient event. Once I had bought the concert tickets, however, I planned my itinerary to the last detail.

1. Be on the plane and leave my hometown at 7:00 am.
2. Arrive in Toronto by noon.
3. During my two-hour layover eat at the airport lounge.
4. Go back on the plane and then arrive at LaGuardia Airport in NYC by 4:00 pm (I'd experienced New York rush hour before so I planned on arriving at the hotel and getting checked in by around 5:30 pm).
5. Leave two hours to eat, freshen up, and walk to the venue, do the meet-and-greet, enjoy the show, and live happily ever after.

But guess what? None of that shit happened. Everything I planned for went into the gutter after I arrived in Toronto.

It all started when the front desk checked me in and mentioned that were would be a delay in the flight to New York.

"How long?" I asked.

"Your flight will be leaving at 4:45 pm," I was told.

That wasn't good news, but there was still hope. I thanked the check-in lady for her time, went to the airport lounge, and sat down to do the napkin math and see if I'd miss the meet-and-greet. If the flight took off by 5:00 pm and landed by 6:00 pm, I could grab my luggage, go to the hotel, drop my bags off, and still arrive at the venue by 7:30 pm. I could make it.

I had three hours in the lounge. I went to the buffet area, grabbed some food and a pint of beer, and got a seat by the window. I planned to have a shower as well before boarding the plane so I would be washed up and looking my best when I met San Holo.

Then the intercom went off.

"Mr. Wong, please report to the front desk."

Thinking it was a call to let me know that a shower was available, I left my food and jacket at the table and headed over to the front desk.

"Mr. Wong," the desk clerk said politely, "I regret to inform you that your flight to New York has been delayed again. We are terribly sorry."

"What time will it leave now?" I asked.

"6:15 pm, sir."

My stomach sank. Fuck. I was going to miss my meet-and-greet. I was disheartened but I kept my poker face on for the clerk because I knew it wasn't her fault.

"I'm curious, what has caused the delays?" I asked.

"There was a pretty bad snow storm in the New York area yesterday," she said. "Most flights were delayed leaving here and there."

When I got back to my seat I googled the weather to see what "pretty bad" meant.

It was an understatement.

The snowstorm was the first really big one to hit the eastern US that year. It was New York's biggest November storm ever, and the city's largest snow dump since 1938.

Wow, Nature had waited 80 years to fuck up my plans. I topped up my beer and started thinking about what to do.

I started going through my emails, looking for the meet-and-greet confirmation email. Then I decided to email the promoter, show them my boarding passes, and explain what had happened in the hope that they could set something up.

Not long after that I received a reply. It said they couldn't guarantee anything if I was late.

That sucked. On to the next idea.

In sales when a customer says no, you don't just close shop and walk away. You look for a solution. I had to think of something

Social media.

San Holo has an Instagram account. 'Why not?' I thought, and I sent a direct message with photos of my boarding passes, my Canadian passport, a screenshot of my message to the promoter, and a note saying I would come straight from the airport to the venue with my luggage. I knew that the worst thing a client can say in sales is, "No thank you." In this case, it would be not getting a reply.

I crossed my fingers, sipped my beer, and waited.

Within minutes my phone vibrated. Someone had messaged me on

Instagram.

I opened up my inbox and saw I'd received a reply from San Holo himself. It was short and sweet.

"You're good bro. I'll see you even if you're 2 hours late. If you're really late, this is my tour manager's cell phone number."

Unbelievable. I'd bypassed the bullshit with the venue and the promoter and not only had I got a reply from the man himself, but he was willing to put himself out for me. All my thinking, fretting, and internal angst evaporated with just one sentence to be replaced by euphoria and renewed excitement.

I believe the moral of this story is that if you care enough and you're willing to put in the effort, you'll be rewarded.

Even though my meet-and-greet problem was solved I still had hurdles to go through. My flight got delayed *again* and this time I was told that I wouldn't arrive in New York until 9:00 pm.

I decided to do my best to send a text message to San Holo's tour manager even though I hadn't been given his name. After some googling I came up with the name Steve, but after I sent a message to "Steve" I got no response.

I messaged San again and this time got a laughing emoji and this question: "How did you get Steve?"

"Google," I said.

"My tour manager is a girl," San replied and gave me her name.

I thought I'd fucked up at that point, but I know how to piggyback on a mistake and turn it to my advantage. Just before I boarded my flight I went to Starbucks and filled two venti cups with as many snacks as possible. I told the barista to write "Steve" on both cups because I thought the tour manager would get a kick out of seeing it. She had an unusual name and people often misspelled it. I felt like I needed to make an impact, and she was doing me a favour by letting me go backstage, so I texted her.

We exchanged a few texts back and forth and I said I would keep her updated about my ETA. Once I was on the plane I sent her a photo of the two Starbucks cups with the caption "I hope you want some snacks." She sent back an LOL and said I should leave the cups at the "merch booth" and she would find me later.

I figured I had won over San's gatekeeper, now all I needed to do was get to the venue.

I couldn't believe how things turned out. This wasn't going to be just a meet-and-greet. Shit, I was going backstage.

I arrived in New York at around 8:30 pm and texted the tour manager to say I had landed and would be there by about 9:15.

I went straight to the venue and when I arrived there was a line up to get through security. I had my big ass suitcase with me so I got some confused looks. Security asked me if I was at the right place.

"I'm here for the show," I told them

"Where'd you come from?" one of them asked.

"The west coast of Canada," I replied. "I had some delays so I had to come straight here with my stuff."

I placed my luggage on the security table and the security person checked the whole thing.

I was so relieved the moment I was finally inside the venue and could hear the music playing. Then I went to find the coat check and had to haul my luggage up two flights of stairs because it was on the second floor. Whatever, I had only a smile on my face.

After I checked my bag, I went to the merch booth, dropped off the snacks in the coffee cups, and proceeded to get to the front of the barricade. Having struggled so much to get there, I was damn well going to watch from the very front. I wanted to be close enough to see and smell the artists. I deserved it.

Two other artists played before San and in that time I made new concert friends around me. When the main event finally happened it was an hour-and-a-half of pure fun and joy.

After the show finished I expected to hear from San's tour manager but no message came. I went upstairs to get my bags but there was a massive line for the coat check so I decided to go back downstairs and wait it out.

Unwilling to give up after everything, I took the initiative one more time and texted the tour manager.

"Hey, the line for coat check is really long, let me know what the game plan is."

I got an instant response

"I'll meet you at merch."

Holy shit. This was happening!

At the merch booth the tour manager stuck out like a sore thumb. Her head was swivelled sideways and she had a clipboard and walkie-talkies on her.

"Hi, it's Wilson," I said when I walked up to her. "Thank you so much for doing this. I really appreciate it."

Then I gave her a hug.

"No problem," she said with a smile. "Now let's take you backstage to meet San."

My heart was pounding. We walked passed more security guards, and I was finally backstage.

Moments later San Holo rushed up from behind me to put his hands into a bucket of ice.

"Hey man, you were so late today," he said casually.

"Dude, I had three delays," I explained.

San extended his hand for a handshake but I asked for a hug. I got it and after that we talked and hung out backstage for about 20 minutes. When it was time to leave, I took a selfie with him, wished him a good night, and we hugged it out again.

As I was walking upstairs to grab my bags, I couldn't believe that any of it had happened. The flight delay looked like it was going to be a fucking disaster but it ended up being one of the greatest things to happen to me, all because I took the initiative in a shitty situation. I learned a lesson I will never forget: don't give up. Never let a circumstance crush your hopes, because you have control over everything.

If everything had gone according to plan on that trip, it still would have been pretty cool. Good thing it didn't though, because when the shit hit the fan, I was able to take actions that turned that night into one of the greatest ever.

Chapter Eight Summary

- When your flight is delayed, ALWAYS milk the airport lounge for what it's worth. Also start with the expensive stuff first.

- Accidentally mess up someone's name? Double down on your mistake and acknowledge the new name you decided to give them.

- Attempt to solve all problems with crazy ideas before you bitch and complain.

- If you want to hang out with your favourite artist backstage, just message them because you never know.

Chapter Nine:

Making Out With Accountability

I have worked in sales for the last 10 years and my favourite thing is attending the three or four major conferences that we have every year. The rule in sales is that you work hard but you play harder. Playing hard is what conferences are for.

Having friends from across the country gather at the same hotel means hours of catching-up after the conference, which usually goes late in the evening. Then everyone finally gets a chance to dress down and go to the hotel bar or liquor store. The veterans will stay up until it's their bedtime, while the youthful souls hang out until 4:00 am. That's when you take a three-hour nap before breakfast and then go to another eight-hour meeting. I love it. It's about quality of time spent versus quantity of time.

On one such occasion I had the opportunity to travel to the US to be a volunteer. The days were long – 7:00 am to 9:00 pm – and then we had to tear down and clean-up. After that I chilled with my colleagues in the hotel room until around 11:00 pm.

Before I left for the US, my buddies back home told me to download some dating apps and make time to go out and meet some beautiful American ladies. I decided to humour them and give the apps a try. I found out they work by swiping on someone's profile. A swipe left says, "Nope, not my type," while swiping right means, "Damn, girl, you fine. Let's talk." The women have to talk to you first, so if you're a super creepy dude, you can't just send a dick pic to them.

Now, of course, I ain't creepy, but I did have a time constraint. So what would this young single male do when he was in a different country with limited time and a dating app? Hey, I like meeting people so…

I perma-swiped right!

I didn't care what race, shape, or size the girl was, or if she had great eyebrows or a unibrow. I laid down on my bed, closed my eyes, and swiped away. I think my finger walked a marathon across that screen.

It turned out that I matched with a ton of ladies (okay, maybe not that many, but I want to give the illusion that every girl in the US wanted to date this Chinese Canadian). A few of the girls reached out to me, which meant I got the chance to talk with some of them.

Once you match with someone you can look at their profile. I got talking to this one girl of Asian descent and she was thick. I love thick girls, and she was Thick with a capital T. She had tattoos, her face was aesthetically pleasing, and she did artsy poses with her friends in front of graffiti. I thought, 'Perfect, this girl seems really cool.' Well, the moment we matched, she texted me saying, "Morning Sunshine. Got plans for tonight?"

It was 9:57 pm, not exactly morning.

'Okay, that's cool,' I thought. 'Don't judge. If she wants to call the evening the morning, I'm okay with that.'

Holy shit though, these American girls move fast.

I decided to be honest with her so I told her I was hanging out with my colleagues and was busy then. She replied, "That's fine," and told me to meet her at a certain bar when I was done.

I figured I had nothing to lose so I said, "Sure, I'll come out tonight."

Fast forward to an hour later and my colleagues are starting to tap out after a long day. They were tired and wanted to get some sleep because we had to be setting up the conference again at 7:00 am.

"Hey Wilson, what are you going to do now?" one of them asked.

"Umm, I guess I'm going to the bar," I told them.

"What? Now? With who?"

"To meet this girl I met on this dating app."

"Wilson, you're crazy. Make sure you're not late tomorrow morning."

My colleagues are awesome because they never judge me. I wished them all a good night and walked back to my room to do a guy's typical bar-night routine: shower, scrub everything, and get game-day ready, just in case.

The bar wasn't far from the hotel and it was a beautiful evening so I took the opportunity to walk through downtown. I love walking through cities at night looking at buildings, seeing landmarks, and watching drunks stumble along the sidewalks.

After about 15 minutes, I arrived at my destination. The bar was Spanish-themed and lively, with people outside smoking and music blaring. It looked like a good place to have a great time. I walked up to the bouncer, showed him my passport, offered some small talk, and went in.

Time to find the girl.

This bar was shaped like a 'B' (think of a capital 'B': narrow straight patch and the right sides were the bar) and I did a quick loop around it looking for a girl with tattoos. On my second pass I saw her from afar.

Here's where things got tricky.

You NEVER know when dating app pictures are taken, and people can change even in a short space of time. Some people get a new haircut, others get thicker. That can be okay as long as the dating app photo looks something like the person you are going to meet. If I look Chinese, for instance, I should definitely *be* Chinese when you meet me. Just saying.

I saw her, I walked up closer, and I squinted (as if my eyes needed to be smaller) to confirm that it was her. Then I did a 180 and walked right out the door.

There is a saying, "When expectations don't meet reality, you'll be disappointed." But I'm a man of my word. When I say I'm going to do something, I do it, no matter what. I promised this girl I was going to see her, so I had to turn up. I just needed some time for self-talk. So there I was, standing outside that bar thinking, 'Wilson, you promised and you're a man of your word. You have to hold yourself accountable. Don't be a flake. Get back in there.'

I knew I just needed to compose myself, because if I met her with genuine interest I was going to have an amazing time. I had to battle my thoughts though. I kept thinking of excuses to tell her why I couldn't make it, or why I should have stayed at the hotel and called it a night. But I couldn't shake off the idea that I was being an asshole. She did not deserve that, and I have integrity (well, kind of at this point).

There was a young guy sitting beside me and I wanted to hang out a bit before I went back inside so I sparked up a conversation with him. He was a student and was waiting for an Uber to pick him up.

We talked for about 15 minutes and as his Uber pulled up I got a text.

"Wya?" it said. *(Where you at?)*

I chuckled. Here we go. Time to just own it and show up.

The bar had a funny vibe that night. It had a very heavy Hispanic theme but since it was almost Christmas, they were playing remixed versions of classic Christmas songs as I walked through the main corridor and passed some heavy black drapes. The moment I walked in, I saw two girls dancing by the door. I locked eyes with a beautiful blonde and stopped right in my tracks. Before I could say anything she walked right up to me, grabbed me by the arm, and started dancing with me.

It was amazing. In the back of my head I was like, 'YES! I don't need to hold myself accountable anymore. I don't need to talk with the dating app girl.' Meeting this blonde was super organic and she was hot. I just wanted to hang out with her (and her blonde friend, of course).

After the dance finished, I did the gentlemanly thing and asked her name. I offered to buy her a drink and we went to the bar.

"I'll get the same thing you get," she said when I asked her what she would like.

"Tequila," I said. "Okay with you?"

She nodded.

After the first shot I needed another hit of liquid courage so I offered to get another round.

"Sure, but I'll get the next one," she said.

Blondie was super attractive, kind, and considerate. I dig that, so I was ready to buy drinks with her all night long. We started with small talk but our conversation got deeper as we got to know each other. She had lived in New York for a while, but moved back home to San Diego where she was a personal trainer. I told her I was from Canada, here for work, and that I wanted to explore the city.

Sometimes it's very difficult to talk to someone at the bar with music blaring, but there are times when I feel like it's supposed to be like that. Loud music makes you lean in closely, face to face. I asked her what brought her and her friend out tonight and she said it was her friend's birthday party!

I turned to her friend and wished her a happy birthday.

She laughed and told me it wasn't *her* birthday. She was just the designated driver.

'Okay, that's cool,' I thought.

Then I asked them if we could go meet the birthday girl and all get a birthday shot together.

We made our way through the crowd towards the bar's back patio. By now I had forgotten all about why I had come to the bar in the first place.

But the universe does not forget. I saw the dating app girl up ahead and we were heading straight for her.

You gotta be fucking kidding me? No way can it be her birthday.

As we got closer and closer, all I could do was chuckle to myself and think, 'Wow, I guess the universe really wants me to own it tonight.'

When we finally reached dating app girl, a.k.a. birthday girl, I had the biggest smile on my face ever.

"This is Wilson," Blondie said.

"OMG, what took you so long?" said dating app girl.

In my head I was laughing, but for an answer all I could do was smile and give her a lacklustre palms-facing-upward gesture and shrug.

"Surprise!"

At this point I decided to own the situation so I admitted to everything. Blondie was confused.

"Wait, you know her already?" she asked.

"Yes, she was the one who invited me!" I responded.

Well now the universe was really going to give it to me. With introductions out of the way, Blondie was whisked away by her other friends, leaving me with dating app/birthday girl. Small talk ensued.

"Hey Wilson, let's go dance," she said.

"Okay!" I said and she grabbed my hand, pulling me back to the dance floor.

At the back of the dance floor was a ledge that separated the dancers from the people walking by. When we reached it she stopped, grabbed the ledge, turned around, and started twerking on me.

'Holy shit, that escalated quickly,' I thought to myself. 'Now, what do I do?'

'Stop thinking, start doing,' I told myself. 'She just wants to have fun and dance with her ass. That's cool.'

When the universe gives you a twerking butt, you gotta grab them hips and just enjoy yourself. I figured my goal now was to show face and have fun, so I did just that.

Not long after, Blondie came back and started dancing on my left side while birthday girl was still twerking on my front. Yep, I was having a blast. I felt extremely confident. Blondie recognised this and moved closer.

I remember a speaker at the conference telling everyone that "Life is too short for small talk." Hearing that in my head, I realised I may not see Blondie again and I wanted to give myself a shot. I grabbed her close and leaned in.

"I just wanted to let you know I find you attractive and I'd rather dance and talk with you tonight," I said.

She abruptly pulled away and gave me a stunned looked. I'd messed everything up.

Then she leaned back in and said, "Give me your phone."

I did as she asked. She put her number in it and we carried on dancing. I must have had a smug-ass look on my face, grinning from ear to ear. I'd never done anything like this before, especially at a bar.

The music then changed to a slow Christmas song and the dark bar lit up. It was closing time. Birthday girl turned around and gave me a hug so I wished her a happy birthday and a good night. Afterwards, I turned to Blondie, gave her a hug, and said I was happy I'd met her.

She smiled and went to find her friends. I said goodbye one more time and went to take a seat at the booth closest to the door. As I watched the bar emptying, I couldn't stop smiling and reflecting on what had come out of my dating app experience. Who would've thought that committing to meeting a girl who didn't turn out to be who I was expecting would make me leave prematurely, then go back in, meet a beautiful blonde, get redirected back to the dating app girl I had tried to avoid, dance with her, and then get the blonde's phone number?

I couldn't stop laughing to myself, but when I looked at the time it was 2:00 am. I had to get back and go to bed because I had to work again in five hours. I stood up and started to walk towards the exit.

Out of nowhere Blondie came back in, her head swivelling, looking left and right. I thought maybe she was looking for something she had forgotten. She then turned, smiled, walked right up to me, and we started making out. It was the best make out session I'd had in a long time. Afterwards we said our goodbyes again and she left.

All of this happened because I held myself accountable. I would never have met this girl if I'd gone home after walking out of the bar. The universe made me own the situation and at the end of the night it rewarded me. Thank you conscience.

Chapter Nine Summary

- Before you sleep make sure you blindly swipe right on any dating app you have.
- You're a person of integrity; always show up when you've said you will. When you see the person you showed up for, run away, contemplate life and then go back in.
- Tequila is delicious but it's also known as liquid courage.
- The universe never forgets why you're there.
- You have my permission to get the phone number of that person you're digging at the bar while getting twerked on.
- Life is too short for small talk when you're in a different country. But when you're back home remember that everyone knows everyone.

Chapter Ten:

Do Cool Shit, Meet Cool People, Do Everything

If there is one piece of advice I would give to anyone who doesn't know what they want to do when they grow up, it's, "Do everything."

Anything you start in life has the potential to have a profound effect on you at some point. When you start on something that is small but enjoyable, you find yourself being able to connect things in the craziest ways. I found this with skateboarding and business.

Some of the other opportunities I've experienced were insane.

Here, as an example, is how I vlogged my way to a job as Events Director with the Front Row Foundation of Canada.

It all started in 2010 when I made a promise to myself that I would travel every year, no matter what. It didn't matter what my financial situation would be or where I was going to be at the time. I made a promise to myself and I was not going to break it.

The year before I had gone to Korea and I loved it. The shitty thing was that I hadn't taken enough photos or videos. I hated that I could only remember a few things after the trip was over. My friends would ask me, "How was Korea?" and all I could say was that it was amazing and I would love to go again. I could mention the *League of Legends* finals and being able to eat some great food, but otherwise I had nothing of substance. I felt like a poor conversationalist.

In 2015 my then-girlfriend and I decided to go to Japan for my birthday. Most of my friends had never been there and wanted me to tell them what it was like when I got back. I didn't want to disappoint them so I thought to myself, 'Fuck it, I'm not going to *tell* them how it is, I'm going to *show* them!'

When I started telling people that I'd vlog the trip, their response was, "I'll totally watch that!"

Having begun building hype about my vlog, I needed a camera. I didn't even have a smartphone at the time, and a camera, it turned out, was really expensive. I thought about my point-and-shoot camera, but even that was bulky, plus I would have to bring a laptop for editing.

Luckily, my girlfriend came to the rescue. She had what was then the newest and latest iPhone4S with a whopping 16 GB of storage. Wow. In 2015, that was amazing technology.

I started playing around with her phone and downloaded an app called Adobe Clip. It was a primitive video editing app where you could literally only do three things: add a video, edit the video, and upload the video to YouTube. I decided that was all I needed to capture our trip to Japan.

The moment our trip began I started capturing everything, from our layover in Vancouver to how much legroom we had on the plane (since my mom is a travel agent I got bumped up to Premium Class). And I didn't slow down after we landed. I documented how we got lost in Japan, where we stayed, what we did, and even how we felt.

When we got back to our Airbnb to unwind every day, my girlfriend would drift off to sleep and I would stay up another hour or two to edit the clips together into a six-or-seven-minute video. I did this every day in Japan for 10 days. We would explore, film and, at night, I would edit and upload. My girlfriend and I would then post links on our Facebook pages. The videos didn't get a ton of views, but that wasn't the point. I did it because my friends and family wanted to see Japan from my point of view.

After that trip was over I stopped vlogging and went on with my life. It wasn't until a couple months after when my friend Will invited me to a Fukienese dinner banquet that I thought it would be kind of cool to vlog again. By this time I had a hand-me-down iPhone so all I had to do was download the app and start filming again.

After vlogging that banquet, something clicked in me. I decided I was going to vlog about something every week. I knew it would force me to leave the house and hang out with my friends. It would also become a time capsule of events in everyday life. I hated writing, so I thought I could journal my experience with video.

Every week after that I vlogged my experiences and travels, and I'm still doing it to this day. I now have over 200 videos on my YouTube channel and I can revisit these memories with the click of a button.

Technology today is amazing. Instead of a bulky video camera like my parents used to use, I can do everything from my phone: shoot, edit, upload, distribute. What that also means is that anyone can do it. I vlog because I can't really describe my experiences to someone, so I want them to see it for themselves. Vlogging makes me zero dollars and I'm not a famous YouTuber. I'm just a dude who wanted to capture his life. You can too.

I did get one big benefit from vlogging though.

In November 2017 my friend Al was a board member of a charity. He and the chairwoman were discussing how expensive it would be to use a photographer and videographer for their events. During that conversation, my name came up.

"Wilson knows how to use a camera and edit videos," AI said. "Why don't we get him to do it?"

He showed the chairwoman a few of my videos and the amount of content I put out. They decided I might be a good fit for the job.

When the chairwoman asked me if I was interested in being the Front Row Foundation's Events Director I had zero clue what the job would entail. I emailed her back and asked for a full job description.

The description she sent me said that my job would be to grant the wishes of people braving an illness, to take families on a front row experience, be social, and have a good time. I would have to make phone calls to venues, hotels, and restaurants to get discounts and then document the events as the photographer and videographer.

Hang on, you want to pay me to travel, which I've committed to doing every year anyway, to be social, to use my sales skills to build relationships with hotels, venues and other places, and to capture moments, which I've basically been doing on my own for the last few years? Does this sound like fun?

Absolutely!

Of course I said yes to the opportunity, even though I didn't know what to expect. One year later I had already granted three wishes, one involving an NHL team in my hometown and two in New York. I'd also gone to San Francisco and San Diego for further education and skills training.

When I started vlogging I never imagined it would lead to granting wishes, traveling across North America, building incredible relationships, and, most importantly, having fun. What this has taught me is that as long as you're having fun, keep doing what you're doing. If you're not, stop doing it.

Here's another example of how I met cool people by doing cool shit because I believe in doing it all.

Since I told you in an earlier chapter how I became, for a few days, perhaps the richest homeless person in Canada, I'm going to tell you now about how I got a new mom and dad.

Through my success in Grande Prairie selling knives, I learned that being client-facing is very important, especially in product and service sales. When I was living in my car I did a lot of appointments, one of which was for a couple named Lana and Greg. I was referred to them by a friend of theirs and I remember calling Lana and booking the appointment.

I recall sitting in the kitchen with Lana's resting bitch face staring back at me. I was young and very intimidated by her. I did the presentation as usual, mentioning my own personal goals to give her a sense of who I was as a person, and then I asked for the sale. She said no, and because I'm not pushy at all, I closed my book and asked if she could give me any referrals.

Unbeknownst to me, Lana had seen the presentation three times before and had never bought anything from anyone. However, before I left the home, she mentioned that she would call me back and buy something from me. I'd been in sales for three years at that point and had heard that many times.

After the summer was over I didn't think anything of it. It's a fact of life in sales that when people say no to you, you forget about them pretty quickly. Though one day in October, when I was getting out of my car at my girlfriend's house, I got a phone call from a number I didn't recognise. Since I'm in sales, I have a general greeting for calls from numbers I don't know.

"Hi, Wilson speaking."

On the other end I heard a bright, friendly voice say, "Hi Wilson, it's Lana. How are you?"

In my head I'm thinking, 'Who the fuck is Lana?'

Then she said, "I'm finally ready to buy."

With that I realised it was the mom whom I'd found intimidating in Grande Prairie and who couldn't be persuaded to buy anything by me or her prior callers.

I was pleasantly surprised. I chatted with her for a few minutes and after we'd caught up she said she wanted the whole package. I was blown away. That was 10 times the company's average sell. I was over the moon and wrote up the order there and then over the phone. It really made my day. I'd made a lasting impression on her. I felt like I was in an MMORPG. I'd raided a dungeon, beat the boss, and got the treasure.

A year after that incident I went back to Grande Prairie to service my clients. I had no idea where I was going to stay while I was there, but I decided to either live at the college again or get a hotel room. I did not need to be homeless this time. Shelter was the least of my worries, so I started booking all of my appointments and eventually got to Lana.

"Hi Lana, it's Wilson. How are you?" I said cheerfully. "I'm calling because your products are due for servicing, and since I'm coming back up to town I wanted to swing by and touch everything up."

"We'd love to have you," Lana said. "Except there's one issue, Greg and I are at the lake house."

"That's okay," I said. "I can come back next year."

But Lana was insistent. "No, no, we want you to come through," she said. "Where are you staying?"

"I have no idea," I said. "I'll figure it out once I get there."

"Okay, why don't you house-sit for us?"

That was unexpected for someone I had only seen once in my life and spoken to twice on the phone. It just goes to show what you can get by building a rapport and openly sharing your goals and aspirations. She knew I had good intentions. Obviously I said yes to her offer.

They gave me my own password to get into the house, then I worked and house-sat. I have now known this family for over six years and Lana has become my mom away from home. After their son and daughter moved away I was even given my own room downstairs with a new bed and some furniture. And did I mention that she is the whitest person I know. I think I'm practically the only Chinese person in Grande Prairie when I go there. I became the adopted Chinese son of this family and even Lana's friends were surprised when she first housed me.

After several years of living at Lana's house, her and I were hanging out in the kitchen one day when I decided to ask her why she had let me into their life.

"Remember how my son plays lacrosse?" she said. "Well when he was playing for other schools, he had billets that he would live in."

I was still confused. "Okay, and…?"

"Well I thought that if my son was doing your job, I would want someone to house him too," she said. "So, here you are."

"Wait, that's it?" I was still a bit surprised.

"Yup, that's it," she answered. "Was I supposed to do anything else?"

That's how I learned what absolute kindness was. This person intimidated me at first and rejected my product, but was still generous when I was in need. Lana wasn't after anything from me. I added no value to her at the time. Yet she decided to take a risk. As a result, I now go above and beyond for her. Whatever product she wants, I let her have either free or heavily discounted. I've become a part of the family and it's extremely rewarding to have such amazing people around me that believe in and support me.

Most of my friends don't understand why I'm living with white folks like they were my own family. When I explain how this all happened, some have said, "There's no way I could do that," or, "I would have just gotten a hotel." I say it's nice to have family all over the place, and they don't need to be by blood.

Now let me talk about this book.

I decided to write this book because I thought it would be fun. However, there was more depth to my rationale than just "I want to write a book." In my sales company, books are often given out at Christmas and birthdays. One of the books that was given to me was *The Dream Manager* by Matthew Kelly. One important idea in the book is that you should write down 100 goals, dreams, and aspirations. They could be anything, simple or ridiculous, such as playing a specific song on the guitar, meeting a famous celebrity, travelling somewhere you've never been, or buying something materialistic.

My list was all over the place: meet Arnold Schwarzenegger, hit a certain level in sales, make my first music album. And jotted in the corner of one of the pages were the three words: write a book.

That list was made back in 2014. Jump ahead to 2019 and you would have found me sitting in a coffee shop writing this book. I wasn't driven by a "new year, new me, let's write a book" kind of mindset. Instead it was a case of recognising opportunity and understanding that being an author is simply living out the current chapter in my life.

Let me backtrack a bit to something that happened with the charity I work for. There was a massive four-day end-of-year event that was being planned to raise a lot of money for the foundation. The events director and I spoke about getting cross-training done so I could help develop a team that would do the same thing that was being done by our US division.

At the same time, the US events director reached out to me and offered me an opportunity to go to a conference in San Francisco about assisted death. This conference would give us a better understanding of our clients who are braving illnesses, and what we can do to have empathy and sympathy. After that conference, the plan was to fly out to San Diego and help run the charity's end-of-year event.

I have a close friend who has over a million subscribers on his YouTube food channel (Don't worry, it will tie back in). Cooking and eating are his passions. We rekindled our friendship after not seeing each other since high school when I bumped into him at a shopping mall. I had seen his cooking videos before and noticed that he used some no-name knives, and since I sell knives, I wanted to give him some of our product.

I didn't want recognition or any product promotion on his channel.

I just wanted him to have some great knives because he cooks a lot and he's living the YouTube dream. Before our reunion at the mall ended I asked him to come to the parking lot with me. We went to my car and I showed him some knives. Then I asked him to make me a list of the knives he wanted so I could get them to him as a gift. He wanted to pay but I refused to take his money. After that we ended up talking in the parking lot for three hours. Our goals and values were the same. It was just a good time to be friends with him again. A month later he decided to invite me into his home to be a guest on his YouTube channel. I was well received by his community and I've been on multiple episodes since then.

How does this story relate to writing a book? Well, on these eating episodes with my friend, we would have conversations and I mentioned my trips to San Francisco and San Diego. People then messaged me on my YouTube or Instagram accounts suggesting places to eat or see in those cities.

I've become a "Yes" man, so when someone reached out to me on YouTube and asked if they could pick me up from the airport, I immediately agreed.

When I arrived at the San Francisco airport my ride was waiting, so I loaded my bags into their car and we were off. That trip turned out to be one of the best I've ever had. The day after I flew into San Diego for the charity's big event, though I didn't arrive until 11:00 pm. Beforehand, I'd asked the event organizer if there was extra room in the hotel, but I was out of luck. On Facebook, however, someone said they had a friend who had an Airbnb that I could use. 'Perfect,' I thought.

When I eventually got to the place there was already a couple in it. I thought they were the owners, but I was wrong. They were there for the event too, and they subletted me the couch to sleep on.

This might sound shady or crazy, but I thought it was the funniest miscommunication about sleeping arrangements ever. Fuck it, I didn't care. I knew I was going to be helping early in the morning and late into the evening anyway, so all I really needed was a place to sleep.

Well, that's exactly how it played out. I woke up every day at 6:30 am and was at the venue by 7:00 am to help set up and run it. Once the day was over, I was there until 9:00 pm cleaning and setting up for the next day.

Because this was a four-day event, there were lots of guest speakers, including people from a publishing company, motivational speakers, and entrepreneurs. I had to sign everyone in and then I could go into the main room and listen. I walked into the publishing company's talk a bit tired and brain dead and was more interested in scrolling through Instagram on my phone than listening. That is until the presenter started talking about how his colleagues were writing books.

That comment piqued my interest. He mentioned that a colleague of his, who was 20, had become a published author and pointed him out in the crowd. I saw who he was and decided I would talk to him about his book. I was curious what he wrote about.

After the talk was finished and the entire room got a break, I approached the man and we connected. He talked about how, as a young immigrant, his life was vastly different in the US than it had been back in his motherland. Eventually he asked me where I was from and I said something general like, "Canada." I assumed most people don't know about provinces, much less Canadian cities.

"Where in Canada?" he asked.

'Okay, I guess I'll tell him my hometown,' I thought, assuming he would not know it.

“I’m from Edmonton, Alberta,” I responded.

“Oh, no way, I know where Edmonton is,” he said.

I was shocked that he knew where my hometown was, so I said the first thing that came to mind, “No the fuck you don’t. Nobody knows where Edmonton is.”

Thankfully he laughed at that and mentioned that a colleague of his, who was also at the conference, was from Edmonton too.

‘Seriously,’ I thought. ‘I need to meet this other Edmontonian. This must be serendipity again.’

I’d walked into a presentation about writing a book, spoken with someone who wrote a book, and was being introduced to another person who happened to be from my hometown and was also writing a book. To me it was a sign.

Call it fate or the universe, but this little voice in the back of my head recalled that list of 100 dreams. I sat down with the two authors and discovered that I lived only five minutes away from the other Edmontonian. At that point I knew that I had to stop dreaming this dream and get on with it. I knew I would never get a better chance to write a book, so I committed. I had gone to that conference just intending to help, but I was coming out of it with a mission. This was going to be a fun way to make money. I always look for the best in a situation so I thought that even if it was pretty bad, it wouldn’t matter because at least it would be a dream I had realized.

That isn’t where this story ends though. The conference was done on Sunday, but I had to stay in San Diego until Monday evening. I needed to pack my shit and leave my sublet couch on Sunday, which meant I was going to be homeless for that evening. Most of my colleagues were flying back home, so I wouldn't even be able to crash on someone's hotel room floor.

It didn't matter to me though, because I figured I would be able to find a bed and breakfast or hostel somewhere in downtown San Diego. I went to the conference Sunday morning to work the event, and after the morning rush I hung out with the two authors I'd spoken with before. I happened to mention that I didn't know where I was going to stay that night and told them the story about the sublet couch. We all had a good laugh at how ridiculous that was. And then several hours later, one of the guys found me and asked if I had found a place to stay that night. I told him that I hadn't even looked.

"That's good, because I've got a place for you," he said.

"Wait, what are you talking about?" I responded.

"I made some calls and got one of my friends who lives on the beachfront to host you," my new friend told me.

"Are you serious?" I said.

At that moment I felt a vibration in my pocket. I pulled out my phone and saw a message waiting for me. It was from the man at the beachfront house.

"Hi, I heard you need a place to crash. Here's my address. I'll see you tonight."

'Wow,' was all I could think.

"Bro, I don't even know what to say," I said to the guy at the conference who had set this up.

"You don't have to say anything," he said. "I got your back."

I was grinning from ear to ear and all I could do was give him a hug.

This was the trip of just letting things happen and saying yes. After the foundation had celebrated its successes that night, I took an Uber to the beachfront house and made another new friend. We had a ton in common and we hung out late into the night talking. The next morning he went to work and he let me borrow his skateboard so I cruised around on it for a couple of hours to explore San Diego. Later that day I packed my stuff, said goodbye, and left for the airport.

That week was supposed to be about work. Instead, I experienced many life-affirming moments. This book was the result of those seven days in California.

When you do cool shit you meet cool people. The "do everything" method pays off eventually, although it might not show up in your finances at first. Chances are though, you'll find a connection that bridges the gap between doing things you want to do and building a financial foundation for the things you enjoy.

Chapter Ten Summary

- It's fun to try new things. If you don't know what to do, do *something*.

- Try to find another mom or dad in a different city. You save a ton of money when you have other parents to live off of.

- Always accept room and board and rides from strangers.

- Everything you do will give you a kickback. Always expect the unexpected, even if you have to wait four or five years for it.

- Seriously, if you do cool shit, you'll meet cool people. So get out there and do your own version of cool.

Chapter Eleven:

The Unglamorous Grind

Every situation, opportunity, or decision I have made has led up to me writing this book, which, on the surface, is a pretty incredible feat. However, when you go a few layers down to who I am at the core, this book is pretty ridiculous and silly.

This book is really just a glorified diary. I wanted to give you a glimpse into my upbringing, my failures, and my successes. I also wanted to open up, be vulnerable, and share my stories because I feel they are relatable. Articulating my thoughts and feelings in the situations I've described has taken more mental energy and memory than I could have imagined.

I decided to write this book because of significant changes in my life. These stemmed from breaking up with my girlfriend earlier this year. That event sucked. A lot. What has happened since though, is what this chapter is about: the process of going from heartbreak to breakout.

One of the reasons why I believe I came out of my situation stronger than ever is because I read many personal development books. Name any renowned self-help book and I've probably read it: *The 5 Love Languages*, *How to Win Friends and Influence People*, *The Compound Effect*, and *The Dream Manager* are on the list with many more. I believe that reading these books saved me from spiralling ever downwards into darkness.

How did it save me?

Through my experience in sales over the last decade I have been brainwashed into thinking positively and holding myself accountable. My mantra is that you have complete control over whether your actions work or not. You can't blame the customer for not buying. You need to look within yourself and see that you didn't have the skills to win the customer over.

By practicing these principles I have learned that if anything "bad" happens to me, my reaction is *always* within my control. When my relationship ended, I went through the stages of grief. I spent two weeks in absolute solitude. I didn't tell anyone. I had to move back home. My mom would ask me why I was at home all the time and I never really answered her. I just shrugged it off and said, "Don't worry about it."

That experience taught me that you should never do that. It's fucking awful. If you are sad, tell someone. Vent and let it out. Keeping myself to myself for those two weeks negatively impacted my emotional and physical state. My sadness ate me up from the inside-out. Motivation and drive were completely sucked out of me. I cried *a lot.* 10 years with someone is a long time.

Through sales I have been blessed to have had access to business coaches and mentors who taught us strategies for selling and maintaining mental health. One of the best things I learned from working in sales and reading self-help books was journaling. For a long time I never really saw the point of it. At one of the conferences I went to however, a speaker gave us an exercise in which we had to jot down one or more sentences three times a day, every day, for two weeks, about how we were feeling. That meant writing something in the morning, afternoon, and evening.

I was in awe of how much of an impact that speaker had. His presentation was funny, genuine, and it made sense. It taught me something that is prevalent in my speech and that I'm using in this book: **use humour with purpose**.

I'm no comedian, but I find everything that has happened in my life to be comical. Being able to go backstage and meet San Holo, getting catfished then making out with a hot blonde as a result, being "homeless" and sleeping by a playground while I'm selling like mad, having an adult hissy-fit and fighting with a paper towel dispenser. To me that kind of shit is really funny. But being able to share these stories is the best part.

Every one of life's challenges that I have overcome has made me stronger than I was before. My job and life have been more grind than glamour, and that's still happening now that I'm writing this book. I live in a constant struggle for continued growth. I feel pretty good at my sales job, but I constantly feel like I'm not capable. Though whenever I doubt myself, it is because I'm comparing myself to 30-year veterans in the business. There is no way I can compete financially with, or have the skills of someone who has been in the business since before I was even born.

Sooner or later playing the comparison game only gets you down. Here's a classic example. Imagine you've just graduated university and got a job in a respected field. Congratulations, that's awesome! However, you see your friends who don't have a degree buying nice things because they had a knack for business, or because Mom and Dad gave them a golden ticket, allowing them to enjoy immediate success.

This upsets you, so you make up a story that because you went to school, you should be more successful than those who did not. You measure success in terms of how much someone travels, what their house is like, what kind of car they have, and what other toys they own. You start telling yourself, "I want that, too. I need more money."

You then dig yourself a hole financially, mentally, and maybe physically. You stop tracking your finances, give in to peer pressure, and start feeling the fear of missing out. You also start racking up your credit card so you can go travelling with money you don't have. You're feeling stressed if you have to wear the same dress or shirt to a party that you wore before. Because you are working more to make more, you start eating out and stop working out. You get fat.

When you play a comparison game like this you live fast, but it's not sustainable. About 0.01% of the population is born into riches or excels in just about everything they do. Most of us will never be like them. If money, status, and material possessions are driving you to make decisions that will make you be like someone you think is more successful, you need to re-evaluate.

The bottom line is don't compare yourself to others.

Of course, this is easier said than done. When you compare yourself to friends, family, co-workers, or anyone else, you fall into the trap of trying to play catch-up. You can't live your best life if you're trying so hard to live someone else's. Real happiness through abundance and success will only come when you stop comparing yourself to another person.

It took me a long time to figure this out, but when I stopped giving a fuck about what other people thought about me, it relieved a lot of pressure. I didn't have to try and impress others, I just had to focus on myself.

If you are living in your parents' basement, don't feel bad because you think your friends have left home like "grown-ups." Be happy that you can save thousands of dollars in rent while you work, and that you get the opportunity to build a relationship with your parents. There is no need to feel ashamed. Personally, I have a wonderful relationship with my mom and dad *because* I stayed at home when a lot of other people my age left to get their own place. Plus I used all that money I saved to invest in myself.

How stressful does it sound to run someone else's race? Stop judging yourself and start creating your own life. If you've read up to this point, you have seen that my life was created by eating a ton of shit and grinding through the unglamorous.

I'd like to talk about a friend of mine who is struggling with the concept of the unglamorous grind. He has been working at the front desk of a gym for almost a year. Initially it was an amazing job. He got a free membership and most of his friends exercised at the facility so he got really fit too. His passions are lifting and videography, so he used the money he saved on membership fees to buy the nicest camera and equipment. That gave him an idea for his first side hustle.

When he originally told me his idea of making highlight videos of competitive lifters and selling them a videography package for their social media, I was so proud of him. He had found a great way to mix his passions at the young age of 22.

As the months have gone by though, his love for the job has started to wane. When you work at a gym, most of the time you are cleaning up after the members. Chalk, wipes, liquids, dust, and dirt, you have to clean it up. Not glamorous at all.

When my friend's side hustle started to grow, his ego began to take over. It started telling him that he shouldn't be cleaning as much as he was, or that he could make more from filming and editing videos. He began to believe the other staff were not doing as much as he was.

I understand that a bit of success can inflate and boost the ego, but in my friend's case, it is not a signal to start disregarding his day job. If he wants his side hustle to grow and become his main hustle, he needs to continue eating shit (or in his case, cleaning it). It doesn't make sense for him to quit or complain about the job that is giving him free access to the people who will use his services.

For him to grow his business, he needs access to people. Because you need more than a friend or two to use your services for it to be a viable business. Getting a business off the ground takes a lot of effort though. Entrepreneurship is not easy or glamorous. My friend is the front-end and back-end staff of his empire. The salesperson, the bookkeeper, the web designer, the video editor, the marketing team, and on the front lines taking the videos and photos. He cleans up after people all day, then has to work late into the night doing stuff that he isn't getting paid to do. But he can leverage his day job to make all that extra stuff worthwhile.

Right now he needs to use his time at the gym as an income-generating networking opportunity. Every gym member that walks in is a potential client. By communicating with members while working he can develop relationships inside and outside the gym, which can make him top of mind as a fitness photographer and videographer. It doesn't matter how many other photographers or videographers are out there in the city. What matters is whether he is in front of potential clients and maximizing every moment with them.

Finding abundance is about searching for opportunities and exploring the options presented to you. Just because you clean toilets doesn't mean you are in a "dead-end job." If you're not having fun, you need to take a step back and have empathy with, and sympathy for, yourself. Why aren't you having fun? What can you do to make it fun? What can you do to make it a learning experience?

Being aware of what you want and who you are is the first step towards figuring out how to make money while having fun. I want to expose you to this because once you know that your mindset and everything you do is in your control, you will have given yourself the best chance to take the bad with the good.

After the split with my girlfriend I felt alone for the first time in 10 years. It took a while, but eventually I came to the realization that we were not getting back together and I couldn't just drown in sorrow. I was still struggling emotionally as my birthday approached, so I called up a friend who is like a sister to me and told her I needed someone to hang out with. We talked for a bit on the phone and had one of those conversations when you feel really sad and talk out of your ass.

"Ugh, fuck sis, I'm so sad that I just want to jump out of a plane."

"Ha ha, you're so funny Wilson," she said and told me she was only about two minutes away.

Right then I had an "ah-ha" moment. I knew I had been talking a ton of shit and didn't really want to jump out of a plane and die. It was just a silly phrase I spat out. But it dawned on me that people literally do that for a living. And then it hit me, why didn't I do it for real, but without dying?

After I hung up, I instantly went to my computer and googled "skydiving near me." I didn't care how much it cost; I was determined to keep my word. I clicked the first link that popped up and searched the company's upcoming jumps. Since my birthday was coming up, I wanted to jump for joy on that day. Unfortunately, they didn't have anything for that date, so I booked a jump for the day before. I paid right away to make sure I kept my word.

When my "sis" arrived I jumped in the passenger seat of her car laughing.

"What's so funny?" she asked.

"Remember when I said I was sad and wanted to jump out of a plane?" I said. "Well, I'm doing it. I just booked a skydive for Monday."

"What the fuck?" she exclaimed. "I was just on the phone with you like two minutes ago."

"Yeah, after you hung up I booked my jump."

"You're fucking crazy!" she said, laughing out loud.

With that act I was starting to take back control over how I felt emotionally. It was tough letting go of the angst and "what ifs?" and the "what could I have done to salvage the relationship?" questions. I came to realizations about the relationship that pushed me to strive for more. Sometimes you just need to flip from one emotional extreme to the other in an instant. Going skydiving was like living those two emotional experiences at the same time. Even though I was sad, I was exhilarated too.

I found out that I would be jumping with a Canadian Veteran who had been jumping out of planes for a living for 30 years. It was to be a tandem jump, so I knew that if I was going to die, he would die too (as a worst case scenario). Reminding myself of this was my way of curbing my fear, because I figured that with his experience the odds of anything bad happening were slim.

On the day of the jump I woke up early, drove to the site, and did my orientation. I then put on my jumpsuit and waited around a while since there were a lot of people ahead of me. In the weeks before there had been a lot of fires in California and the smoke blowing north into Canada had caused many jumps to be postponed until the day I was jumping.

When my turn came I was calm but highly energized. I felt a

mixture of sadness and elation at the realization that I was about to jump out of a plane. I also knew that I needed to go back to work that afternoon.

The plane was a tiny 1969 Cessna that took only five people. The interior was ripped out for maximum space but it was still very intimate. It took about 20 minutes to get to the jumping altitude of 10,000 feet, and during our ascent I was gifted with some spectacular views. There was no turning back now. I was jumping out of this plane one way or another.

When you are high enough that houses look like ants and the subdivided land looks like a patchwork quilt, a lot goes through your mind. I thought about the work I needed to do after the jump. I thought about how loud the engine was and how rickety the door of the plane was. I thought about the past weekend and what I wanted to eat later. I thought about everything.

I had butterflies in my stomach, but I was still very calm and had a bit of bravado in my system. Though when they finally opened the door and all I could hear was the BRRRRR-BRRRRR of the propeller I had an "Oh, shit" moment. I was in a tiny ass plane with the doors open at 10,000 feet and about to jump out.

I tiptoed onto a metal foot rest and then sat down on the edge of the door, ready to go.

"ALRIGHT LET'S DO THIS," shouted my jumping partner over the noise. "HOLD ON. THREE, TWO…."

And we jumped.

The initial feeling of falling lasted just a few seconds. We did two front flips and then it was gone. What followed was the coolest feeling in the world. It reminded me of riding a motorcycle. That extreme sensation in those moments made me forget about literally everything. It didn't matter what had happened in the past or what I needed to get done later that day. I felt present in the moment. This was real, everything else was just thought.

It's easy to spend too much time in your head overthinking and over-analysing. But when you’re falling at 190 kilometres an hour there is nothing going on in your head. A mix of fear, euphoria, and joy overwhelm everything else. It’s exhilarating.

Then the parachute opens. Words really can’t describe what that feels like, but I'll try. Although I was gliding through the air, it felt like everything was in slow motion. The air was crisp and clean and I had free movement of my arms and legs. My ears were a bit cold from the altitude, but I had 360 degrees of viewing pleasure. There was no obstruction to my view of the clouds above or the farms and homes in the distance below. It was the most rewarding and liberating experience I’ve had. Gliding through the sky was so peaceful and quiet that I could feel and hear my heartbeat.

As we approached the ground, any feelings of sadness or worry were wiped from my thoughts. I acknowledged that they were not gone forever, but they did not inhibit my ability to move forward with my day. I felt truly at peace with my situation and myself. Even now it seems crazy that my committing to something based on an impulsive sentence I said when I was feeling down would lead to such a life-changing moment.

The only person who knew that I was going skydiving was my “sis.” I didn’t tell my mom or dad because I knew what they would want to know first.

“How much will it cost?”

I told them about it after the fact and my mom’s response was,

"What?! $300 to jump out of a plane? Why didn't you let your dad drive you down the highway with the windows rolled down and you could have paid for the speeding ticket!" My dad just thought I was crazy.

Sometimes things don't turn out the way you think they are supposed to. That applies as much to work and business as it does to relationships. Having the mindset to come to terms with this is something we all need to constantly work on. Just because you have a photo with your significant other on Instagram doesn't actually mean you're in a happy relationship.

Equally, you might think you have a successful business, but life can suddenly kick you in the throat and you'll need to deal with it. Sure, you can put on a brave face every day for the people around you because you're petrified of being judged, but when you get home you'll find yourself asking, "What the fuck am I doing?" and have to figure it out.

Whatever extremes you go through, remember that your feelings are in your control. It's okay to be sad, but catch yourself when you are aware of how you feel so you don't dwell on it too long. Snap out of it. What was the craziest thing you've always wanted to do? What's something that people never thought you could do? Do it to change your direction. Make it your breaking point, where you will change your way of thinking and act to make it better.

When you do this, something happens to you. You forget about your woes and problems because you focus on the task at hand. You've shocked your system, forcing the change and breaking through the limiting mindset you had for yourself before.

When hope starts fading, we feel weak and hate ourselves for living that way. So don't pretend that it's going to be alright. When you accept who you are, you can move forward. It is not easy, and it's not going to change overnight. It could take months or even years. It doesn't matter though. Once you make the change and commit to the unglamorous grind, everything you achieve will not only humble you, but make you proud of yourself. What you accomplish will let you realize that you are capable of being an incredible human being.

Up to now in this book I've been sharing with you my struggles for success. Being the son of working class immigrants means it was never going to be an easy journey. There were moments when I felt fear, uncertainty, and doubt. Some challenges beat me down, but I always I ended up facing them with a smile, even when I didn't know what to expect. I was yearning for others to believe in me. I wanted to be the best. But I had to learn the best way to get the support that I needed.

The journey of entrepreneurship, like jumping out of a plane, was something I couldn't turn back from once I committed to it. Secure long-term abundance was what I was chasing. Call it the Canadian Dream. I was on a pilgrimage for my idea of success.

The unglamorous grind is watching everyone pass you by while you move towards your goals. It is the ability to set those goals and have absolute conviction that hitting them is the only way. It's about being able to reflect on how ridiculous and hilarious the journey can be. It's about having the mental fortitude to keep doing what you're doing even if there are no results for months or years, working tirelessly on skills that open doors of opportunity everywhere you go. It's holding yourself to the highest level of accountability and knowing that to you, your word is absolute and binding. It's the ability to sustain positivity and enthusiasm even when you fail over and over again.

The day you decide to accept that the grind will be shitty is the day you stop worrying about the opinions of others and rely on your ability to take action, develop skills, and find the abundance you've been craving.

Chapter Eleven Summary

- If you say you're going to do it, you'd better do it.
- Break-ups suck, but self-loathing is even worse.
- If you bitch and complain a lot, nobody will want to hang out with you.
- Go skydiving. It's good for your health.
- Keep eating shit if you want to succeed. Just don't get used to the taste.
- The grind isn't always glamorous, but you can be proud of yourself for the actions you've taken.

Chapter Twelve:

Monetize Fun

Wow, I've made it to the final chapter of this book. I actually managed to sit down and write all these words.

You've made it too, so I want to thank you for taking time out of your busy schedule to read my stories. I hope you've enjoyed them and now have a sense of why I feel like my life has been ridiculously fun.

To wrap things up, I want to give you some perspective on what money and fun could mean to you. Focusing on having fun doesn't mean you aren't taking life seriously. It just means you aren't taking it *too* seriously. Working your ass off to put extra zeros at the end of your paycheque isn't necessarily going to bring you fulfillment and joy, so you need to find those where you can.

How did that happen for me?

It was trial by fire. My parents wanted me to get a white collar job like a doctor, lawyer, accountant, or teacher, since those sound like good jobs to have on the surface. Though as I grew older I started asking why they wanted me to have that kind of occupation. My mom eventually admitted that it didn't matter what job I got as long as it wasn't back-breaking work. I applied to be a landscaper for my first summer job and they said absolutely not.

I wondered why my parents were opposed to this type of work. I thought it would be great to be outside, enjoy the weather, and make money. They explained that this kind of job was not something they wanted for their son. They travelled on a boat to avoid the Vietnam War and came to a free country so they could make sure I had all the opportunities in the world. They didn't want me to be a labourer, they wanted me to have the education they never got, and to use it. To them, anyone can lift a sack of rice and put it on the back of a truck. They believed that if I received a Western education, I would do more with my life than pick things up and put them back down.

They romanticized white collar jobs because clients would come to me rather than having to entice people to purchase a product or service. My mom is a travel agent, so people go to her if they want to go somewhere. Doctors will always have patients and teachers will always have students. In these types of jobs, life would not be "hard" because you would never be short of clients.

It makes total sense why immigrant parents want their kids to have the top service jobs. When you've taken the chance to escape all the problems of a developing country and come to a place with seemingly unlimited opportunities, it would be crazy not to take advantage of those opportunities.

As the previous chapters have explained, I never did get the kind of job they wanted me to have. I threw myself into sales even though my parents didn't like it. Sure, I got to "suit up" and go to conferences and look nice and professional. But sales is not an "easy" career. For one thing, you need to have motivation, belief, and conviction to sell a product. And second, it's not stable, it doesn't pay a salary, and you have to find your own clients so you can pay the bills. That's pretty scary. Sales means pressure, and pressure, to my parents, means "hard."

Often it is the closest people in our lives who are our biggest critics. "Don't do this, don't do that." "That's crazy, you shouldn't do it." Yet if you stop listening, run your own race, and find success, those people come back into your life.

If you're surrounded by negative people though, you need to get the fuck out of there. And the best way to "get out" is to be aware of your situation, accept it, and change it.

We've all had friends that are flaky. They are really annoying because you never know if they will show up or bail at the last minute. Don't cut these friends out of your life though. Acknowledge that they are like that and accept it.

Also consider that maybe it's not your friends. Maybe it's actually you. Ask yourself if you're the flaky one. Don't be one of those friends who talks a lot of game but never acts on it. If you want to change, talk the talk and walk the walk. At first it's going to be a challenge and you won't see instant results. However, over time, something is going to click and then the change will happen exponentially. And keep a record of it so you can be inspired later.

As an example, I track my finances on an Excel spreadsheet. I journal about my emotions and feelings. I take videos to document my progress through my journey. When I get a chance to look back at my videos or my finance logs, I think it's incredible how much I've done. Thanks to my finance journal I know everything I spent in the past five years. When I look at my YouTube channel, I see that I've made over 200 videos about things I've done. It's amazing to look back and see how I committed to things and saw them through, or how small decisions led to big accomplishments. If you keep enough of these records, they will help you to start recognising opportunities.

When you start early with something, the experience you get from it will compound overtime. This may sound crazy, but just starting something you've dreamed of, whatever it may be, is the same, in principle, as someone choosing to leave their country to seek a better life elsewhere. It shows you that through the force of your own will, you have total control over decisions that will move you forward.

When you choose your path and don't allow someone else to choose it for you, your eyes open and you gain new experiences that no one else can get. These turn into skills, and when you combine experience and skill, especially when you're young, it means you not only recognise opportunities, but have the smarts to act on them. Then opportunities start popping up out of nowhere.
x
Why is that?

Because the skills you develop unlock the ability to recognise opportunity. Regardless of whether you make money or not, doing something you want, and the fun you have, opens doors. That is the most exciting part.

Often people who go into something they enjoy don't do it for the money. Before they made it big, most of the world's amazing artists, singers, actors, and musicians had to put up with answering the question, "What bar or restaurant do you work at?" There are many more people, meanwhile, who will never make it in the arts, but the skills they gain from their efforts will transfer over to another role that they can excel at. Something is always gained if you have the right mindset.

I have an engineering friend who makes a lot of money. One time I wanted to go to an event with him, but he was working *a lot*. I asked him what his schedule was like and he told me he had worked 26 days out of the last 28 and he was on night shifts. That made me wonder if the older guys who had been working in his field for years were now pawning off the shitty work shifts to the younger guys, believing most young guys will take them because they want the money.

Young guys, like my friend, who accept this have a great work ethic, but it's not a great life ethic. Working non-stop from age 20 to 40 before you can finally have fun doesn't sound appealing to me. Yes my friend makes mad cash, but I've lost him to the grind, and he truly doesn't enjoy what he does.

Working like my friend just to pay the bills doesn't give you the ability to recognise opportunity. Imagine you are an actor with bravado, confidence, and charisma. You also have a real-life superpower: you are great at memorization. You can memorize any script, recite it easily, and it becomes a part of you. What kind of job could you do where you can use this skill, make money and keep working at being an actor so you have fun?

Sales.

In sales you need to speak with confidence and be able to network, so you can develop these skills – the same ones that will help you be a better actor – while also making money. It doesn't matter if you sell homes, sauce, or widgets. Use your skills to their maximum potential to make money and have fun while working towards your dream.

Here's another example. You've dug yourself into debt because of your love of fashion. You have more clothes than a store could ever hold. You're working part time trying to pay off your debt, but your mind keeps wandering to your love of fashion. How can you find fun in your situation and monetize it?

What superpower do you have that will bring you joy and help you make some coin?

Since you're a fashionista you may know the places that get the best discounts, deals, and exclusive brands or items. There's an opportunity: start writing or vlogging about that. It's free, and it's stuff you're doing anyway so you might as well track your journey. Why not approach a modelling agency too? You get to take photos of amazing clothes, 'gram it, and move on to the next trendy wear.

You have more clothes than most people, so why don't you flip them or put them on consignment? Better yet, ask someone who trusts and values your skills in fashion if you can sell for them and get paid a commission for doing so. Then you'll get the best of both worlds: you get to wear other people's clothes without paying for them, and you become the expert. It's always fun to do the thing you want to do and have people pay you for it. You just need to be open to opportunities beyond what you can imagine now.

Whatever you're doing, if you're having fun, there will be opportunities to monetize it. Some ideas may be practical, others wild. Yet, when you start looking for opportunities, somehow they start showing up in your life. You might think it's the universe smiling on you, but really, it's you. It happens because you have worked on expanding your skills and training your mind to start seeing things differently. When you do these things, you're putting yourself ahead now rather than later.

To achieve this, speedy decision-making is extremely important, and that in itself is a skill. There is no "maybe." If you sit on a decision all night, you've probably already missed the opportunity. This doesn't mean you're impulsive; it shows that you can take action the moment you realise you have a potential opportunity in reach.

As an example, I am going to refer back to the breakup with my girlfriend. After the relationship ended a lot of my friends sent their regards or invited me out to get my mind off things. My friend AI had invited me to a social gathering on a Sunday night that started at 9:30 pm that I agreed to go to. But when the time came to actually leave I was at home and said, "Fuck, I don't want to go out." But since I'm a man of my word, I went.

I had two choices that evening: be the flaky friend and say, "Nah man, I'm tired. I don't wanna come out. It's late and I have work tomorrow." or commit and say, "I'll see you soon." I had to make my choice on the spot because if I waited, I would be late and maybe even miss the party. So I got my ass out of bed and drove straight there.

I didn't know what to expect when I arrived at AI's place, but it was buzzing with energy. As I walked in I could hear music, laughter, and conversation throughout the house. I'd been there before so I knew there was a custom-built taproom in the living room with six taps that offered seemingly unlimited beer. This was the environment I needed to be in during my time of sadness so I am forever grateful that AI invited me. I pat myself on the back too, because I would have missed it if I'd been lame instead of deciding to go.

As the night progressed I met more and more people and I found out that they all had one thing in common: they were in the beer industry. I got to hang out with brewmasters from several top restaurants and craft breweries. I was among some of the most important people in the beer scene. These were the guys who actually make the beer.

Earlier that afternoon I had talked with one of my old assistant managers from the sales company I worked for. He helped me process my break-up too, and we got into talking about business. One thing he told me was that at the end of a conversation you should ask, "What can I do to help?" I didn't think anything of it at the time, but I would discover what a great question it was later that day at Al's party.

At one point I was being a wallflower and listening in on a conversation between two brewmasters. One of them was talking about how amazing and tasty the Green Tea Saison beer he made was and the other was asking him questions about how it was brewed. I didn't understand all the lingo but what I saw was two passionate nerds getting a super hard-on over beer.

"I would have made it this way."

"Oh man, I tried it that way before and it botched my entire batch. That's why I did it this way."

"Wow, I wouldn't have thought about making it that way? How did you figure that way out?"

I didn't know what the fuck they were talking about but I did know this: they were sharing knowledge, they were passionate about what they did, and they were making money having fun.

As I sat there, it also dawned on me that I wanted to be a part of this amazing culture. To the guys at the party, brewing beer was never about money; it was about finding ways to make it better and support the local craft beer community.

After running hundreds of interviews, hiring, training, and recruiting people at my sales job, I recognized that here was an opportunity for me to be a part of this beer thing. Before the night ended I chimed in on the conversation and discovered one of the brewmasters had just opened up his own brewery. I asked what the brewery needed and whether he needed someone to help out there. The brewmaster's passion came out when he answered me.

"Aww, man I wish we had more tanks. It would make my life easier."

I kept that in the back of my head, thinking it might pay to recall it later.

The more I listened to everyone interact with each other, the more I had a desire to get involved. Here was a passionate brewmaster who was following his dream sitting in front of me. I knew from my experience that sometimes you just need someone who believes in you.

I was behind him wholeheartedly. I believed he could become the best of the best. At the end of the night I thought of that question my former colleague had told me to ask: "What can I do to help?"

At first the brewmaster brushed it off, but I was adamant that I wanted to support him because I believed in him. I recognized his dream and I wanted to help him achieve it. Before he left that night I made sure he gave me his phone number so I could set up a meeting with him.

A few weeks later we were sitting down at a restaurant getting to know each other. I asked him how he would feel about me purchasing a new tank for him. It was a risky move on my part to give a complete stranger money, but I knew he was a genuine person. He was hesitant though, and asked me why I wanted to help.

It was simple, I told him, I wanted to help because I believed in him. That's all there was to it. He still didn't understand, so I explained to him that his interaction with the other brewmaster was the most inspiring conversation I'd listened to in a long time. I shared with him that in sales it's very difficult to get other people to believe in you because you're in a job that is not stable. The best way for me to show my belief in him, I said, was to put my money where my mouth is. It was a risk I was willing to take because, whether the business failed or not, I wanted him to know I *truly* believed in him. He didn't accept anything from me that night, just paid for my beer, and he said he'd keep my offer in mind.

A few weeks later we met again at the same place and started talking about his brewery. This time he opened up a little more and admitted that he'd asked AI if I had just been pulling his chain. AI vouched for me and described me as "good shit."

Now that the brewmaster trusted me he went for the ask.

"We don't need a new tank," he said. "However, we do need these chemically treated floors because of the chemicals and the clean-up required to clean the tanks. Without the floors the cement will get eaten up and that will cause long-term issues."

"Cool, how much are they?" I asked.

"Well if we got someone to do it for us, it would be really expensive," he told me. "However, this guy said he'll teach us how to install them and it would be dramatically cheaper."

"Sure, let's email that guy right now and I'll pay for it right away," I said.

"Wait. What do you mean you'll buy it right now?"

I pulled out my wallet and took out my credit card. "I said I'll help you, so let's do it right now."

"Are you serious?" the brewmaster asked.

"Yeah, I am," I said. "Let's do this and try to get a discount."

So, I bought the floors for the brewery that day having only met this individual a few times. Now, almost a year after that, the brewmaster has become a very close friend, I never have to pay for beer again, and I get invited to really cool parties and events.

It was never my intention to get any benefit from helping the brewery. Rather, my belief in the brewmaster was solid, and I wasn't sure that he really believed in himself. Also, I had no doubt in my mind that my investment would be paid back one day.

If you have a goal and a vision, you're passionate about what you do, and you're having fun doing it, you will attract people who will support you and want to see you succeed.

If you are still growing up and you don't know what to do yet, that's okay. I didn't plan to be a knife salesman or write this book. Everything leading up to those experiences – the hardship, the heartbreak, the passion, and the grind – taught me what is important in my life. I love having fun, it's as simple as that. However, I'm doing it in a way that means I own it and nobody can take it away from me. If you're absolutely certain about what you want, you can have it no matter what other people's opinions of it, or you, are. I wanted to have fun and make money, and I am doing both.

Remember, just because you don't achieve something right away doesn't mean you won't achieve it at all. If I could do anything in the world, I would love to play music. To get there though, I am taking a different path. It's a bit slower, but I'm definitely enjoying the ride for now. I have built a strong foundation in business and entrepreneurship, I have developed strong relationships, and I have given back to the community. I know that because of these, one day I will be paid for my skill and expertise pursuing my dream of making music.

The monetization of fun is whatever you want it to be. Sit down and write out what is fun and even funny to you. The fact that there are people out there making memes for a living is crazy. Everything that you have a passion for can be shared through the internet. It can be monetized globally.

If you have the same mentality as me, maybe you can monetize your fun by being outrageous and ridiculous. When I think about what I do for a living, I find it really funny. I sell knives to real estate agents to supply them with closing gifts. What kind of job is that? It's about as niche as niche markets get.

That's not all I have though. I started a YouTube channel because I wanted to show, not tell, my friends about my vacation. I get to grant wishes for a charity to people in difficult circumstances. I wrote a book because if a 20-year-old can do it, so can I. I wanted to be a part of the beer industry and now I'm close friends with people in it. And on top of all that, I've started my own coffee company because I didn't want to buy coffee from other people anymore.

Everything can be monetized. This book is a glorified journal about having fun and making money. I had a ton of fun writing it and now, when someone purchases it, I'll make money. So I monetized my fun.

How can you monetize yours? Read books, go to workshops, pick experts' brains, and, above all, believe in yourself. Do everything in your power to achieve the fun you desire. Don't half-ass it. If you're going to have fun, do it right the first time.

Take the initiative, hold yourself accountable, work hard, be resilient, and have the positivity to laugh things off. These were the building blocks I used to develop my skills to make money and have fun. It won't come overnight, but love it or hate it, if you work hard every day, you'll see opportunity everywhere you go.

There will be a time when you're so excited to wake up every day to tackle the challenges ahead, you'll beat the alarm clock. You will have a roaring crowd cheering you on and people that you can depend on. You will have fans of your accomplishments and you will inspire others to follow your example. Then, when night comes round again, you'll be mad at sleep for taking you away from the fun you're having. That, to me, is a great problem to have.

Final Chapter Summary

- Don't spend ALL your money on stupid shit. Just enough.
- If someone tells you can't, do it anyways and see what happens.
- You have my permission to drink on a Sunday night.
- If you believe in someone, tell them, show them, and support them.
- Give yourself permission to monetize your fun.

Acknowledgements

I want to thank Angie for truly believing in me when I didn't believe in myself.

Mom and Dad I love you both. Thank you for raising me and letting me do whatever I want.

To my brother, thank you for making me a more sympathetic and empathetic person.

Lana and Greg for being the best home-away-from-home parents. I dedicate all of my successes in Grande Prairie to you because you decided to let a random Chinese guy housesit for you. Geri for being the best Grandma away-from-home. Jackie, Monica, and Leanne for supporting me from day one.

Shout out to my entire Vector, Alumni, and CUTCO family. Who would've thought that selling knives would change my life. Jordan, Mitch, Angie, Denise, Joe, Vonny, Baptie, Chloe, Alex, Jarrod, Mike, Rachelle, Shefsky, and Fiddler.

I'm blessed to be a part of the Front Row Foundation organization. I want to say thank you to everyone that is involved. To Helen and Bex for putting up with me during our events. To Alexa and Nicole for being the strongest people I know.

Shout out to my AB Craft Beer family, Andrew, Dalen, Matt, and Taylor.

If it wasn't for the *Best Year Ever [Blueprint]* event, this book would not exist. Thank you for making my dreams come true.

Musical shout out to: Ilan Bluestone, San Holo, Orjan Nilsen,

Alpha 9, Lane 8, Above & Beyond, Cosmic Gate, Periphery, Post Malone, and Morgan Saint. Y'all don't know me, but the thousands of hours I put into your music helped me write this book.

My New York Family at The ROW NYC. Jojo, Grace, Aleks, Ronny, and Eliane.

To Eric Lim (aka DJ Limit). Thank you for taking me on an incredibly fun journey. I will never forget about it.

Shout to my homies for being there for me when it mattered the most. Jodi, Jacky, Ryan, Will, Kehrl, Evan H, Jeff G, Devin, Simon, Sapna, Jonni, Quang, Duy, Alokin, Oriana, Edwin, Rachel, Arty, Immy, Anna, Joshua, Daisuke, Sandra, Avery, Kassi, Eden, Evan L, Eddie, Connie, Hai Au, Treena, Maryann, Alex, Tania, Jeff P, Mark, Jessie, Kenny, Bella, Alexa, Jelesa, Justin, Isaac, Warren, Grace, Alvin, Kelvin, Kelly, Jessica, and Cindy.

To my past girlfriend for being a beautiful person and making me a stronger person today.

Finally, thank you for reading the entire book, even the acknowledgments. There's nothing left for me to share. You can stop reading now and go have fun. Byeeeeeee.

You're still reading?

This is my self-promotional page. You can slide into my DMs.

My Instagram is: wilsonwongisepic

If you want to watch my journey, I upload on my YouTube channel weekly.

YouTube Channel: Wilson Wong

I'd like to hear from you. If you have an amazingly fun story, please email and share it with me.

Email: wilsonwongisepic@gmail.com

Enjoyed the book? Go on Amazon and leave your review.

Fun is my Favourite F-Word

Made in the
USA
Middletown, DE